Life, Luck and Lancasters

Warrant Officer Louis Butler DFM.

LIFE, LUCK AND LANCASTERS

Vivid wartime reminiscences of
Louis Butler DFM
Warrant Officer, Wop/AG RAF, retired

Christine A. Butterworth
with
Susan C. Butterworth

HENHAM BOOKS LTD

© Christine A. Butterworth 2013

All rights reserved. No part of this publication may be reproduced, stored in a retrieval system or transmitted, in any form or by any means, electronic, mechanical, photocopying, recording or otherwise, without prior permission in writing from the author.

First published in 2013

British Library Cataloguing in Publication Data

A catalogue record for this book is available from the British Library.

ISBN 978 0 9576155 0 2

Edited, designed and produced by
Priory Ash Publishing
2 Denford Ash Cottages
Denford
Kettering
Northants NN14 4EW
www.prioryash.com

Published by
Henham Books Ltd
118A Shaw Road
Rochdale
OL16 4SQ

CONTENTS

1	Joining up	7
2	Getting serious	19
3	Among the best	32
4	Hit	48
5	Testing times	58
6	The luck of the draw	68
	Postscript	73
Appendix 1	Operations flown by Sqn Ldr Locke's crews with 467 and 463 Squadrons	74
Appendix 2	Extract from 463 Squadron Operations Record Book, November 1943	75

Author's note

This book is based on transcripts of recorded interviews by Louis Butler's daughter, Christine A. Butterworth, and his grand-daughter Susan C. Butterworth.

Additional editing by Simon Fowles.

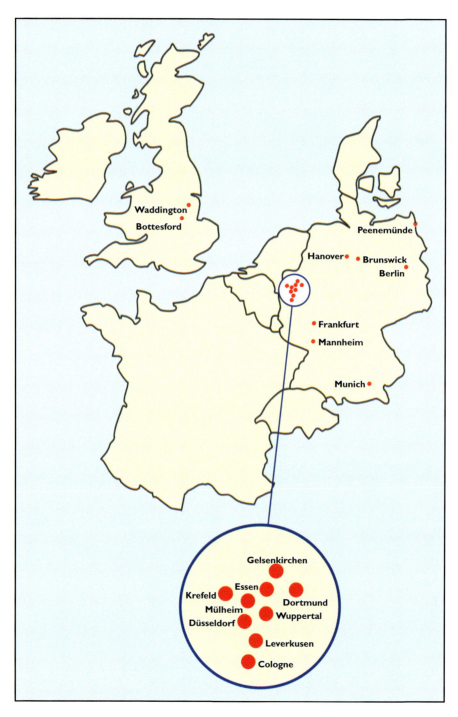

German destinations of raids undertaken by 467 and 463 Squadrons

1. Joining up

This is Louis Butler, aged 22 years, flying for the first time in the RAF in the year 1942 from Yatesbury, an RAF signal school in Wiltshire. I was there training for air signals, and was learning to be a wireless operator/air gunner.

The first time I flew from Yatesbury, which had just a small grass runway, was in a Dominie, a civil version of the Rapide used for air ambulances in Scotland and flights to the Isle of Man. It was a biplane, holding six or seven pupil wireless operators with a corporal instructor and a pilot. The pilot had been taken off operations and was flying Dominies from Yatesbury during a rest period. He was absolutely bored out of his mind.

On board the aircraft there would be six or seven sets of equipment that we had to operate as trainee signals pupils. We had to receive and send messages to the local station with just a short-range set while the pilot flew in the area, and had to do exercises under the instruction of the corporal. We would start sending out about eight words per minute, because the keys were very, very tightly sprung so you could still send messages when the aircraft was fluctuating, moving up and down and bumping about.

I remember the first occasion that I had to receive and send to the local station – our own aerodrome. I was in the throes of sending back a message under instruction when the pilot, who lived away from the camp with his wife, started circling in tight turns over his own house with his wife waving below from their garden. He was just bored, so started doing these tight turns while I was attempting to send Morse at eight words a minute. It was impossible to do this against the 'G' and the strength of the aircraft as he turned so tightly. My hand was just jammed to the key and I couldn't send anything: all I was doing was sending a continuous signal. Of course, on the ground, they didn't realise what the pilot was doing, and when I landed I got a report back which said, 'Big improvement required in sending Morse,' though this had not been my fault at all.

A typical situation in the Dominies when there were seven trainees up there and it was the first time anyone had ever flown, was that it was ten-to-one on that one of you would be sick. When you were queuing up waiting to take your turn to fly the Dominies you would inevitably see one trainee coming off the last flight holding the biscuit tin. He would be the one who'd been sick and it would have also cost him half a crown to pay the ground crew to clean it out when he got down. Nearly every time you landed there would be one bloke emptying the biscuit tin!

After training in Dominies, we were promoted to flying as the wireless operator with just a pilot in a single-engine aircraft – a monoplane. It was very small, a Proctor, fixed undercarriage, and the pilot just had to fly at around 1,000 to 2,000 feet while you went through your exercises. One of the main things was to reel out your trailing aerial, which was on a distress frequency. We had to practise going from a high frequency, which was a short aerial, then changing our transmitter and receiver over to medium frequency, to which the trailing aerial was connected. Inevitably, you were so busy when you were doing your exercises before you landed back, completing everything, that many times the trainees left the trailing aerial sticking to the edge just as they were coming in to land, forgetting to reel it in. There again, it was another half a crown – or five bob – you had to pay for losing your trailing aerial; even though they gathered them back, you still had to pay out. Just another of the hazards of the early flying days as wireless op trainees in the air force.

It had not been a difficult decision to join the Air Force. I wanted to volunteer before but I was in the butcher's shop with my mother and she wouldn't agree to me going. When I was 20 I had to go and she couldn't stop me. And that is when I volunteered for flying duties. All flying duties personnel were volunteers: Bomber Command or Coastal Command, whichever you were, aircrew were all volunteers.

As I said, I'd fancied joining the Air Force before, but it was one night in particular that convinced me. On Sunday nights I used to go with a few of my pals into a pub called The Alexandra on Park Road in Oldham. We always used to go in there, this crowd of lads all about the same age, and one Sunday we heard a great commotion. It was 1940 and the Germans were bombing Manchester. We went to one of the highest points in Oldham, called The Lows, to see what was happening. The aircraft were going straight over the top of us; we could hear them although we couldn't see them. They were bombing and in the distance we could see Manchester burn. That made me want to join the Air Force to get our own back. In December 1940 that's what I did. It was around the same period when they bombed Coventry, which was absolutely devastated, a complete wreck. They bombed the cathedral and everything.

I joined, and as it happened I was sent into Bomber Command, which was doing all the bombing of Germany.

After I had taken the normal fitness test down in Manchester on Dover Street I saw an RAF officer and applied to go into the Air Force.

I passed A1 physically, and a while later I was sent for. It was 30 December 1940 and I was sent to Padgate, an RAF station near Warrington. There I had an aircrew medical, which was more severe than the ordinary A1 medical, and an interview for aircrew, which was special.

I passed to train physically and to train as a wireless operator. The only thing was, I was sent away on deferred service because they hadn't the equipment or the instructors to train us immediately, and you had to wait your turn to go. I was given this slip of paper to say that I was on deferred service and would be sent for in due course, which turned out to be six months later, in July 1941.

There was the normal training that any military man had – square-bashing, learning how to fire a rifle and all this sort of thing. The rest of the time was spent in learning Morse. We were training in Blackpool in what was the Winter Gardens. It was set out in tables with a wireless instructor, who was sending Morse, and there would probably be somewhere in the region of about ten people to each table.

From there I passed out. And the funny thing about that was that you had to pass out at 12 words a minute and you were allowed, I think, a couple of mistakes. You took the test above Burton's, the tailors, in Blackpool. That's where you got the saying 'going for a Burton' from, going for that test. It was set out with a table at the front and a warrant officer sending the exams – the plain language and code in Morse. Everyone was shaking and frightened to death of going. I failed the first test, and if you failed you had a fortnight's deferred service where you learned a bit more about Morse, then you took the test again. It was a terrible fortnight.

When I passed the second time and I went to the warrant officer's office in the Winter Gardens, he looked it up and said, 'You passed the first time.' I had had a fortnight of worrying about it when I hadn't failed the test at all.

It was a great feeling; you really felt you were doing something. It was quite an important position to get from being just a butcher and leaving school. I had gone to elementary school, then straight into the family business, but I enjoyed the change. It was interesting and also a challenge. You felt that having passed out you had really achieved something because you had learned quite a lot in a short space of time.

After leaving Yatesbury, and having successfully passed the course as a flying radio operator, my next flying episode was to go to gunnery school, which was a six-week course at Pembrey, near Llanelli in Wales. There, we had to fly in Blenheims. They were more or less obsolete for operations but were used for the training of air gunners. They had just one turret, a mid upper turret, and you would fly with one pilot and three trainees and probably an instructor. But we used to have to take our turn in the turret to fire our number of rounds. In the mid upper turret there were just a couple of handles to rotate the turret or depress or elevate the guns. The bullets would be blue-tipped, red-tipped and green-tipped, and you knew the sequence in which you were to fire from the aircraft; you were either first, second or third.

Alongside the aircraft would be a Lysander towing a drogue, like a white, fairly long windsock, and we had our instructions to fire at this. There were two Browning guns that fired 3.3 ammunition, which was the same as that used by the Army in a Lee-Enfield rifle. The Browning guns were very efficient, firing a tremendous number of rounds a minute. Each trainee had to fire his particular colour at the drogue and was instructed in deflection. We were told that the bullets didn't fly straight but flew in an arc, allowing for the wind and the drift. You had it all lined up and had a sight on top of your Browning, a sort of illuminated circle with a dot in the middle, and you fired at the drogue, which wasn't a great distance away, probably 200 or 300 yards. You obviously hoped, when you got down, that you'd hit the target. You were firmly convinced you had because when you landed you had to run, pick up the drogue and put it on a long table to see how many hits you had. If, for example, you were 'blue' you were looking for a blue mark on the drogue. But it was always a waste of time because there was never a mark on the drogue. We just never hit the thing. I don't know how this was because you were always convinced you'd had a number of hits. It was unbelievable! To hit the drogue looked so simple, but I don't think anyone ever hit it.

I remember one occasion very clearly. I was called out just as I was having my lunch and told that I would be flying in half an hour. I was only half way through my lunch and for once I was enjoying it. It was a bit like a roast dinner with chips, carrots and peas, quite a pleasant meal in fact. However, I dashed down to the aircraft and we started flying. But the aircraft obviously had a leak in the hydraulics and every time you lined yourself up to fire at the drogue the turret seat sank down and the gun's controls went up, making it impossible to fire at the drogue. The seat in the turret kept sinking because of the leak. On this occasion it was very turbulent. We were flying over a river estuary and there was a lot of bumping and banging and, suddenly, all my dinner came back, all over the guns. I had carrots and peas in my shirt, on my tie – everywhere – because the wind was blowing in through the gap in the cupola were the guns fired from. You can imagine what a mess I was in and it wasn't really my fault because they hadn't given me time to have my lunch. This was another of the joys of flying.

I did quite well from my stay at Pembrey. After passing out I was recommended for a commission. However I didn't get this. When I went in front of the selection board I reacted as though I was suffering from an inferiority complex, so didn't interview well. In fact, the only one of us recommended who actually got the commission was an elderly bloke – at least, to us he seemed elderly. The rest of us were turned down.

So from there I went on to Kinloss. This was an OTU (Operational Training Unit) on the Moray Firth in Scotland, east of Inverness, where I was going to get crewed up and then sent to Bomber Command. When you left gunnery school you either went to Coastal Command training stations or Bomber Command training stations. Up at Kinloss they were flying very big, old, very slow and under-powered aircraft – the Whitley – which was known as a flying coffin because of the altitude at which it flew. It was more like flying a square box than an aircraft, but it was reasonably safe.

I arrived at Kinloss and for the first two weeks we had ground instruction. As wireless operators we were being taught all the various aspects of Bomber Command training and each individual member of the crew had a fortnight's training in his own trade – the bomb aimers, the navigators, the pilots, the gunners. In that period we met people and had to sort ourselves out to get 'crewed up'. I didn't know anybody and hadn't a clue who to ask for advice. But one day I was just wandering between the classroom when two chaps came up to me. One was an air gunner and the other a bomb aimer. One said, 'Are you crewed up yet?'

'No,' I said. 'No, I haven't sorted anything yet.'

'Well,' he said. 'We think we've got a pilot.'

It turned out that the pilot was an Australian. He was a pilot officer with a commission in the Royal Australian Air Force and he looked a very reasonable sort of a fellow, so the four of us got together and decided that what we needed next was a navigator. Unfortunately, it looked as though all the navigators had been taken, when along came someone who said there was one navigator who hadn't made it on the last course as he had been forced to go home before finishing the course because his wife was ill. When I met the navigator I thought, I don't know about this. Most of us were young, aged between 19 and 24. The pilot, the bomb aimer and myself were between 20 and 23; the rear gunner was older, 31, which was quite old for Bomber Command, but this navigator was 33. And when we saw him, to us he looked about 50. But he turned out to be one of the finest navigators in the Air Force – at least we thought so. He was brilliant. We found this out especially when we got out on operations.

So that was the crew as it stood. There was the rear gunner, Tommy Munro, 31, who had trained in Canada; there was myself in the aircraft as wireless operator; the navigator, Horace Hassall; and the bomb aimer, Frankie Townsend, who had trained in Canada at the same place and time as Tommy Munro. They had both gone over there as pilots and been regraded to bomb aimer and rear gunner. The pilot was Harry Locke from Australia. There was no mid-upper gunner on the Whitley.

We all got on well together and continued our training and flew daytime, first of all, with a staff pilot on cross-countries in an Avro Hanson – a very safe aircraft. They used to call it a flying greenhouse because it had so much glass above the cabin where the crew sat. I had the job of winding the undercart up, about 150 turns. It was worked by a mechanical winch.

I always remember the first time we flew in daylight. It was bright sunshine and, believe you me, from a wireless operator's point of view the sunshine wasn't very helpful. When you tuned your radio from your transmitter you had to do it by switching on your transmitter and your radio, then pressing the Morse key on your equipment so that you got a signal coming from your transmitter to your receiver, which was what you called a Magic Eye. This would glow green and you had to close it up so you were on frequency. Well, you can imagine, if it was bright

Harry Locke's Lancaster crew from 463 Squadron at Waddington in January 1943. Left to right, they are Louis Butler (wireless operator), Horace Hassall (navigator), Frankie Townsend (bomb aimer), Squadron Leader Harry Locke (pilot), Tommy Munro (rear gunner), T. Brook (mid-upper gunner), and Bill Holt (flight engineer).

sunshine, which it invariably was when you were flying above the clouds, you couldn't see the green as the sun just blanked it out. It just looked grey. The only way you could tune it was to roll a piece of paper like a funnel, put it to your eye to look at the Magic Eye, press the key with your elbow and try to tune it with your other hand. You really needed the tentacles of an octopus to do it.

On our first cross-country we all underwent a variety of exercises in our own fields of expertise. The trip took about 3 hours over the north of Scotland at about 4,000 feet. We then flew 'circuits and bumps' and did take-offs and landings. Whenever a bomber took off in Bomber Command, either training or not, it always had to carry a wireless operator. It didn't matter about the others, although, obviously, there had to be a pilot. This was a safety precaution so the wireless operator could always get in touch if the RT went U/S (unserviceable) or any such thing. He could always help with the navigation. So during the circuits and bumps training, whether day or night, there always had to be a wireless operator flying. You flew in turn, but there might be two pilots and one wireless operator.

I do remember waiting to fly on one occasion and watching a wireless operator I had got to know quite well go flying take-offs and landings with two pilots, taking off out over the sea. I saw his flight take off towards Findhorn over the Moray Firth. That was the last time we saw or heard from them. Instead of coming round and coming back into land they just went straight into the sea. We didn't know whether the problem was caused by a technical fault or by human error, but the plane went down and we never saw them again. This was one of my first experiences of the dangers and trauma of flying in Bomber Command.

I also remember the first night we moved as a crew into a billet. We moved billets after the first fortnight from a big house a few miles out of Kinloss, which belonged to Thompson, the publisher. It was a tremendous mansion, but we only used it to sleep in. It was November and we would cycle to the camp for all our meals, then cycle back to sleep in the evening.

When we moved from there it was to a satellite place just outside the drome called Forres. As we moved into a large Nissen hut, a crew was going out to fly a cross-country on their first night without a staff pilot. I remember it well because we had only been in the hut a couple of hours when we heard this tremendous explosion from the hills above us. The aircraft carrying the crew had crashed into the mountains just outside Kinloss and they never returned. It was their first and last experience of flying as a crew.

Eventually the time came for our crew to take on our first daylight cross-country without a staff pilot. This was a big moment and everyone knew they had to be on the ball. Although it was a bit nerve-racking, we progressed quite well. We had a 4-hour flight and went through all the right procedures, remembering our technical training. I was using the radio and transmitter, receiving and sending signals to the station. The bomb aimer went through the ritual of bombing as we carried practice bombs. The rear gunners had to simulate aircraft attacks and the navigator had to make sure we were on track.

When we returned to the camp I had to go through a procedure with the pilot called 'descent through cloud'. I got in touch with the ground station by WT as we approached; I pressed the key and they directed me onto the station. Even though it was daylight, it was done as though there was cloud and we couldn't see the drome. We had to go over this exercise even though the ground was clear. When I pressed the key they gave me courses through which to steer into the camp. I passed these onto the navigator, and he told the pilot which course to take. As we approached the station we went onto RT and were told to go round. Once we had broken through the cloud we came in and landed as normal. Unfortunately, however, the pilot hadn't realised what was happening. He thought that when we were given instruction to land after assuming we had gone through cloud he was just to go in and land. By doing this he was going into land at the wrong end of the runway and, as luck would have it, we were going in to land just at the moment a staff pilot and crew were taking off at the other side in an Avro Hanson. We were therefore coming in at one end as they were going out at the other.

I can tell you at that point we had a few very anxious moments, but it was lucky for us that, just as we came in to land, the staff pilot in the plane going out had the presence of mind to pull his Avro Hanson over the top of us, taking a steep climb above us just in time.

The flight offices were at the entrance to one of the hangars, which was parallel to the runway, and the wing commander in charge was in his office watching all this, while jumping up and down going mad. My pilot went in to see him when we landed and he got about three strips torn off. He was lucky that as a crew we weren't taken off altogether. It was actually a tactical thing. Our pilot had got the wrong impression of what he was supposed to do. Instead of going around and landing normally he just came in when I told him to, instead of coming in at the proper runway end. Again we had experienced a few moments of trauma! From then on, however, we sailed through the training.

After that episode everything was fine until we came to fly on our first night cross-country without a staff pilot – another hair-raising experience. We did the cross-country flight just great, but when we got back to camp the weather was really atrocious. It was a squally night with rain and sleet as we were trying to come in to land. There was one hell of a cross-wind as we tried to come in, and the Whitley, with its large wingspan, was not the easiest of planes to land. It was soon blown off course; with hailstones and rain, visibility was very poor. It was really a very frightening event because each time we tried to put the wheels down the wind was trying to blow us off the runway and onto the boggy land at the side. We went round three times and I was getting to the point of thinking we would never get down. The plane was going up and down, swinging sideways and rocking like a cradle. However, to our great relief, after circling for the third time, the pilot managed to bring it down on the deck. Considering it was his first time handling a big bomber like that he did a marvellous job because the conditions were horrendous. Thank God we got down, to everyone's relief.

That was our crew's first experience of flying at night time without any instructors with us. So we had a fair breaking-in, really.

We continued with all the instructions and training that we had to go through, but I think that incident made the powers-that-be decide we needed a bit of extended training, so we were sent to Cornwall to fly Whitleys over the Bay of Biscay. There was a detachment there, and they sent crews for six weeks down to St Eval, which was on Coastal Command. The nickname for it was 'Kipper Fleet' and for six weeks we flew as a crew on Coastal Command, flying Whitleys across the Bay of Biscay looking for submarines. It was all part of the course here, although we had very little armament, just two Brownings on the rear turret and one Vickers gas-operated gun that fired 500 rounds out of a front turret. Above the bomb aimer we also carried two depth charges. We had extra petrol tanks in the fuselage and I had the job of going through a very narrow tunnel between the crew compartment, which housed the pilot, the navigator, the bomb aimer and the radio operator, and changing the petrol over from one tank to another. In the fuselage they put extra fuel tanks so we could go straight across the Bay of Biscay and back, as far as northern Spain. I had the job of connecting these tanks in the fuselage because, as wireless operator, I was the nearest. In this little tunnel there was a cubby hole with a lever that had to be turned 150-200 times to transfer the petrol into the tanks in the wings of the plane. It was quite a job because it had to be done on your hands and knees. You hadn't much room, and by the time you had finished you were sweating even though it was cold. However, it was worthwhile because the extra fuel meant we could make the return journey to northern Spain and back, on average 10 hours, which was a long time flying in a Whitley.

My job was generally quite easy when we went on these trips. I would collect the rations in a big canvas bag, similar to the bags newspaper boys carry, although a bit wider. In the bag there would be five biscuit tins containing each crew member's rations. There would be sandwiches, blocks of chocolate, barley sugar and a flask that would contain Oxo, tea or coffee. I used to spend the morning helping myself to whichever I fancied, then I'd pass the sandwiches and the flask along. It was quite a reasonable ration; we were away for 10 hours so we needed something substantial.

I had at the side of me a small window from which I could look out on the ocean. I had two sets in front of me, called the Marconi 54/55 – the 54 was, I think, the transmitter and 55 was the radio. I had to tune the transmitter to the radio so I could transmit if I needed to, then at the side I had a Morse key. I took a broadcast every half-hour to keep in touch with base and, in between, the navigator would ask me to get bearings. We had a direction-finder on the top, which was just a round aerial that could be turned through 360 degrees. You could tune in on a station and, by looking at the calibration underneath, you could see what bearing you were from that station. If you could tune it in strongly enough, you could do the direction-finding on such stations as Bordeaux or Corunna. There were different radio stations playing music, and tuning into these would give the navigator the bearing; flying over the sea we had no sort of pinpoints. All we could do was take wind drifts off the froth on the top of the waves. Apart from that we just had to go on dead reckoning and the navigator had to navigate to the best of his ability.

As a check for his position, he wanted to get these bearings from the various stations on the coast of the Bay of Biscay, down France and Spain. I used to get these bearings and give them to him, and he immediately threw them away. I won't tell you how he swore when I gave them to him because it became obvious that the continent was occupied by the Germans. They weren't going to let us navigate off their stations, so they bent the beams. How they did it I don't know, but they used to bend the beams somehow when they sent out the broadcast, which meant that you couldn't use their signals for navigation purposes. But my navigator didn't seem to appreciate this and took delight in taking it out on me as if it was my fault.

On these trips I'd take the *Daily Mirror* with me and make the best of it while it was daylight. It was rather a boring trip. The thing was, we were flying at approximately 2,000 or 3,000 feet, maybe a shade higher, and all we were doing was looking out for submarines with our bare eyes. The Coastal Command Whitleys had all the equipment, electronic sets, etc, which helped in the search for subs. It used to get very boring looking at the waves when there was nothing there. Occasionally you might see three frigates or three destroyers sailing over the rough sea, bouncing up and down, and I used to think, well, there's one thing, I'll be back having my breakfast with bacon and eggs and you laddies will still be on the way, a thought that cheered you up as you went along.

On the technical side, we carried these two depth charges in the bomb bay, the idea being, of course, that if you saw a submarine you would sweep down as fast as you could and drop your depth charges where the submarines were going to submerge. To be honest, the chance of sinking the submarines was pretty slim because a Whitley was not very manoeuvrable; it was very slow and all you could do was put the nose down and descend as quickly as you could to drop your depth charges. But by this time, even over 2,000 feet, I think the submarine would have been well away. I think our biggest job was flying from England to Spain and back, and therefore if any submarines were on the top they would submerge automatically if they saw an aircraft. Maybe, in that way, many times when we didn't even see a submarine we were helping the convoys by making submarines submerge when they didn't want to, therefore using their batteries, etc. If they had to submerge they couldn't do a lot of damage. So that was our effort towards winning the war in the Atlantic, which lasted for six weeks.

2. Getting serious

We were billeted at a very good place called Treyarnon Bay. We were flying from St Eval and we were billeted out in somebody's summer residence on the side of a beautiful bay. There was a natural swimming pool outside in the rocks. It was a lovely spot and there were only six crews there. We had our own civilian cook, and our own little bar and snug. It was very pleasant although it was early in the year, but it was miles from anywhere – the only trouble with the whole thing. Anyway, we did our six weeks there, then we expected to move back to Bomber Command and on to whatever they had lined up for us, possibly the Halifax, Stirling, Wellington or Lancaster. But no, being typically military, they did the unexpected.

They sent us away for a fortnight somewhere up in the hills. I still don't quite remember where it was, but it was just above Grantham. It was a bit wild where we were and they sent us on a commando course, which I can't say we really appreciated, particularly our navigator, Horry, who was 33. He wasn't altogether au fait with PT and such things – it wasn't his forte. Anyway, we survived it.

One thing I do remember was that we would just get out at night to a nearby village pub. I heard that there were two ladies that kept the pub and one of them was Stan Laurel's sister. When you went in there was no doubt about that whatsoever – she was the spit of him.

From there we moved on to Winthorpe, not far outside Newark. It was a Heavy Conversion Unit and it was converting from Whitleys to Lancasters. Well, that made our day! That was *the* aircraft we wanted to fly in. But again, we were slightly disappointed because the first thing they did was make us fly Manchesters, which nobody liked to fly. Unfortunately, the Manchester was a long way from being anywhere near as enjoyable as flying a Lancaster. The Manchester was made at

Avro's before the Lancaster and was its forerunner. It tended to yaw across as you were taking off and landing, and there were a lot of accidents. They did fly on ops but they had a very poor record of survival. They had two great engines, which were really two engines in parallel in one nacelle, and this didn't seem to work. The tail plane had three fins, a middle fin and two outer fins. The layout inside was similar to a Lancaster, although it didn't fly anything like it. Our first flights, day and night, were in Manchesters – then we converted to Lancasters. What a difference!

What a fantastic aircraft the Lancaster was. It had four Rolls-Royce Merlin engines, one of the main features of the change, and a redesign of the tail plane. It was unbelievable that you could have an aeroplane that could be so much better than its prototype. From then on we flew in Lancasters and we never ever criticised them as an aircraft, nor did anybody that I ever knew who flew in Lancasters on operations for Bomber Command. If you speak to any member of the air crew who flew in them you will find that they all hold them in great esteem. To stand and listen to a Lancaster go by, the sound of those four Merlin engines, even to this day sends a thrill up my spine. It is a fantastic feeling.

At Winthorpe I recall one particular incident. We were lined up outside this classroom where we were having all sorts of lectures and training before we went on operations and moved to a squadron. A wing commander came outside and he had a black dog with him. He started to talk to us and took us in the classroom to give us a lecture on crew co-operation, how to discipline each member of the crew with the pilot and the captain of the aircraft, and how to behave when you were on ops. The way you disciplined yourself was a sure way of helping you to survive. You certainly wanted everybody to do their job in a proper order, and know how to use the intercom to speak to each other and so forth. It wasn't until later that he became so famous that everybody remembers him. Gibson … Wing Commander Gibson … the leader of the Dambusters raid. This was in May 1943 and it was only a week or two afterwards when we opened the paper and listened to the radio about the great Dambusters raid. This was 617 Squadron in 5 Group.

We were sent from the conversion unit to a place called Bottesford, a little village I had never heard of. The railway line is on a run from Grantham to Nottingham, and just to the side of it is the Bottesford aerodrome. I think we were sent there because my pilot was Australian (the only Australian in our crew) and it was 467 Squadron RAAF, a Royal Australian Air Force squadron. I would say there was possibly no more than half of the pilots who were Australian, and maybe the odd

Above The unmistakable outline of a Lancaster in flight. This is the Battle of Britain Memorial Flight's Lancaster PA474, seen here in the colours of QR-M 'Mickey the Moocher' of 61 Squadron, which she wore until 2006. It is one of only two airworthy Lancasters in the world, the other being in Canada. MoD, *reproduced under the Open Government Licence v1.0*

Below This composite photograph shows the interior of a Lancaster. On the left is the wireless operator's table with the Morse key bottom centre. Above is the Marconi 1155 receiver, and above that the Marconi 1154 transmitter, which worked on a number of different frequencies. Looking down the plane, the navigator's table can just be seen, positioned sideways facing the port side. At the front there is a temporary seat for the engineer. The bomb aimers sat below while the pilot and aircraft controls were above to the left.

smattering of a gunner or navigator here or there. The rest were mainly British or other empire air crew who made up the RAAF squadron. Of course, as time went on more RAAF people came over, but when we joined it the vast majority were British.

When you left from either OTU or 'Kipper Fleet' and came to convert to Lancasters, your crew then increased from five to seven – a flight engineer and upper gunner would join. You needed the extra two crew members because you had an extra turret for the mid upper gunner and you needed the flight engineer as the pilot couldn't possibly keep an eye on all the meters and equipment himself. The flight engineer acted as second pilot and sat in a temporary seat next to the pilot. He helped to make sure all the engines were running properly and the transfer of cocks for the petrol, etc. Some of the flight engineers had experience of flying, but the majority had been ground engineers who went on a course to convert to flight engineers. They had not usually had much experience of flying, so they were thrown in at the deep end on operations, which I felt was a bit unfair.

We then started to fly Lancasters from Bottesford. But before you started on operations you had to fly so many training flights again. You think you are ready but, no, you still have to carry on getting training and instruction. So, on the first flights the pilots were doing circuits and bumps on Lancasters and wireless ops such as myself had to fly with them. Then we did the odd day cross-country and they would see the record of the navigator and check everybody, weigh up the crew and so on. The last thing you did before you went on operations was to fly two or three what they called 'bull's eyes' – simulated bombing raids, but over Britain. They were of a duration of about 4 or 5 hours flying at night, and the whole thing was done as though you were on operations. You'd do so many bombing runs in different places, simulated bombing runs, and the pilot would have to fly straight and level, open the bomb doors, and the bomb aimer would simulate dropping his bombs. There would be areas where the gunners would have to practise in various ways. In some of the major cities in Britain they had been pre-briefed and all the services attached to them were geared up as though they were being raided by enemy aircraft.

I remember the first one, which showed the inexperience of my pilot at the time. We were flying over Hull and the searchlights were coming up. I was listening out to Group broadcasting every half-hour. Suddenly I went off my seat and rose in the air into the astrodome, which was just above my head. My spare accumulator came up and hit me in the face, then we dropped back again. I wondered what the hell was going on. The pilot had actually taken his eyes off his instruments to look down at the searchlight. He'd taken his eyes off his artificial horizon and I thought we must have done a roll or something similar. We continued this operation, eventually going to Hull, Liverpool and one or two other places, then came in and landed after 4½ hours.

I got out of the aircraft the usual way, out of the crew compartment at the front, over the bomb bay, then dropped down to the back door on the left. Just before the rear turret there was a ramp that the rear gunner used to slide down into his turret, closing the two doors behind him. When he came out of that rear turret he'd slide back up the ramp and climb down through the back door. At the side of this ramp was the chemical toilet, and when I looked up there was a mass of slime and oily stuff on the roof of the aircraft and all over the floor. It must have tipped onto the ramp, so when the gunner came out he smelled rather evil. We wouldn't let him come on the little coach that took us back, but told him to wait for another transport and shoved him back. He wore a yellow suit that was electrically insulated, as it was very cold in the rear turret. But the yellow suit was brown all over. That was the proof that we had rolled the aircraft and it was a good lesson for the pilot. I don't think he ever forgot his artificial horizon after that. That was one of our first instances of flying in the squadron.

After that it got serious. This was what we had been training for since 1941 at Ground Radio School in Blackpool for the initial training and elementary radio, then on to Yatesbury and Pembrey, the gunnery school. From there on to OTU, then 'Kipper Fleet', Winthorpe conversion unit, and finally to the squadron. Now it got really serious.

It was the first operation and it was 23 or 24 May 1943. The target was Dortmund in the Ruhr, the big industrial centre in Germany. That was where all the manufacturing and the large producers of munitions were based, as well as the various other components that made up war machines, particularly in Essen, where Krupp's was probably the largest munitions manufacturer in the world.

Each morning you would go down to look at the operations list. If you were listed for ops you would say to your mate, 'We're on tonight,' then you would get a feeling in your stomach like butterflies that would stay with you all the time. You were keyed up, you would go in for a briefing with your own department, and you were briefed by your signal leader. The bomb aimers would be briefed by the bombing leader and the pilots would have their own briefing. Then you would go into the main briefing. You would all sit at tables and on the platform in front would be a big map of Germany and the whole of the continent. Across it would be a red ribbon going from your station, probably doing a cross-country first, which would take up the best part of an hour because to get to Germany you couldn't get the height unless you did a short cross-country beforehand. So you probably had three legs on the red ribbon.

We crossed generally in the region of the Wash from Hunstanton, very often going across the coast at the same point. Some were just below the Wash and some over it – it varied. The Ruhr was an industrial area very similar to Lancashire, where you have towns such as Blackburn, Burnley, Bolton, Oldham and Rochdale. This would have been just as big a target to the Germans as the Ruhr was to us. At that period it was called the Battle of the Ruhr, and this was our first trip, Dortmund.

At the briefing would be the group captain, the squadron commander or wing commander, flight commander, squadron leaders and the Met officer in charge of the weather. An intelligence officer would tell us what we could expect in terms of the heaviest fortifications and the biggest resistance to our raid, fighter attacks and so on. The wing commander would tell us what the target was, what time we were taking off, which wave we were on, the directions we were going to take, the heading into and out of the target, and all the various bomb loads that we were carrying. Generally, we carried a 4,000-pounder, which was called a 'cookie'. It was the shape of a canister, a hell of a size, and we would be carrying six or more 1,000lb bombs made up with cases of incendiaries.

After the briefing was the worst time, as you would usually have a couple of hours to wait around. Part of that time would be taken up by 'the flying meal', when we were usually treated to an egg and flying breakfast type of meal. We would eat this, then sit reading the papers in the mess. Then the time would come to go, and all sorts of wagons would come up, what they called utility coaches, which would hold about 20 men. If you didn't get on a coach you would get on the back of a wagon. These would take you down to the flight although sometimes you would have to walk there. When you arrived you would go into the locker rooms and put your flying clothing on.

I sat in the warmest part of the aircraft. The heat ducts for the plane, particularly for the forward cabin where all the crew were apart from the two gunners, supplied the heat. You could vary these ducts and increase or lower the heat. This caused a constant battle between the navigator and myself because he would say he was sweating and ask me to turn the heat down, but then, when he turned away, I'd turn it up again as I was cold. I didn't wear special flying clothing, only my parachute and harness. I only wore ordinary boots because I always thought that if I did come down and wanted to escape I would have a better chance in these than in the flying boots they gave me, which were big suede things.

I was once diverted when I was on Coastal Command. We landed in Beaulieu, Hampshire, and were allowed to go into Bournemouth one night. When I got back to the local station I had to walk a mile and a half to the camp. My socks were worn out with walking in the flying boots and I thought there would be no chance I would ever escape if the plane came down, so I never wore them on ops.

The gunners, however, needed all their flying clothing. They had tailored suits that were buoyant in case they came down in the sea. They were very vivid yellow, which was the colour for air sea rescue, and they were electrically heated. They were lined and plugged into the turret to get the warmth. They also had electrically heated gloves that kept them comparatively comfortable, but they were very bulky when they got in the turret. It didn't give them much room. The pilot and possibly the navigator and the bomb aimer would wear their Irvine jackets and their flying boots because the bomb aimer could be pretty cold up front and the pilot wouldn't be very warm. They would wear more or less all their flying clothing, except the parachutes and harness. The pilot had a special parachute, which he sat on. His seat was hollow and his parachute and harness formed his seat. If he did have to vacate the aircraft in an emergency he already had his parachute attached to him; it would have been a bit bulky and awkward getting out, but it was there. The rest of us put them in a special storage point so they were handy if needed.

Next we would go out to the plane, one of the worst times of all. There could be anything from 20 minutes to half an hour before take-off and each air crew would find its own plane at dispersal points around the drome, all waiting for the moment of take-off. Occasionally, a van would come out and the driver would tell you there had been a delay, so you might have to wait another half-hour before take-off. That was even worse. The mood was always sombre before take-off because we all knew we were taking a risk. We were losing mates all the time. The actual number that finished a tour was roughly three out of ten, so you knew you were taking a big chance every trip you took. Once you left the coast you were always at the risk of fighters and ack-ack over the target. You were in hostile country and you were always on your toes, and when you got back it was a great relief.

But then the moment came and you were ready to go.

The ground crews would bring the portable accumulator and plug in; this was used to start the engines so you didn't use up your own electrics and batteries. They would start the outers, then the inners, until all four engines were running. Everyone checked their positions. Earlier in the day we had all done an air test. We had taken the plane up for half and hour and we had all checked our positions and all our equipment.

Then we were ready for take-off and started taxiing out. It was quite a sight to see the perimeter track around a bomber aerodrome, as each aircraft came off its dispersal and joined the queue round the airfield. One by one we came to the end of the runway.

At the flying control caravan, the duty officer in charge would get word from the flying control tower at the start of the runway. There was no radio communication whatsoever because the Germans were always listening in. Once the operations were on, there was absolutely no use of radio at all. A green light would be flashed to go, red to wait, etc. When you got the green light you'd be revving your engines up, and the brakes would be on. The rear gunner and the mid upper would come back to a crash position just behind the bulkhead where I sat, then we were ready for off.

I could see out from my position in the astrodome. There was always a group of airmen and WAAFs waving you off and wishing you the best of luck. The pilot would have the flight engineer next to him, who would then start pushing the accelerator knobs forward to slowly set off. 'Full boost,' he would say, and as we gradually gained speed the tail came up. We would take off at around the 100mph mark. It always seemed to just clear the fencing at the end, but then you were airborne. You would settle down, getting in position for the journey, as we continued across the North Sea to the target.

On our journey to Germany we could see the enemy coast was coming up, from somewhere in the region of 15-16,000 feet, and we would be still climbing all the way. We always tried to get to 22,000 feet if we could. If it was a good aircraft you would get there, or if not you may get to 20,000 feet or sometimes only 18,000 feet. But you were always hoping to get to 22,000 feet to put you above the rest. Very often you would see Halifaxes and Stirlings over the target area. They always seemed to be a bit lower down than us. I always felt that when you were dropping your bombs it was much better to be above rather than below.

All the way from the coast you were gaining height, more or less until you went on your bombing run. You would start to see the flak coming up as you flew along, especially over Holland. You would go over the North Sea and come to the Hook of Holland where there would be all sorts of ack-ack. Then you would go over the water where the Hook of Holland is and hit the main coast, and there would be more flak. There were flak ships, which used to throw all the muck up. The raids were planned to try and avoid them as well as they could, though this wasn't always possible. Many times you had to go through the flak, which was a good distance from the target. Once you'd cleared the coastal areas and it quietened down a bit you had the problem of wondering if there were any fighters about.

Everybody was always on the look-out. The two gunners and the bomb aimer would be looking out and I used to get in the astrodome and look out when I wasn't doing the broadcast. Being the wireless op I was often cut off from the intercom, and had to receive any messages from Group every half-hour. This could take quite a lot of time and often you weren't in communication with the rest of the crew until you tuned yourself in. As the wireless op I could switch myself in or out of the intercom depending on what I was doing with the radio.

I had to get half-hour broadcasts and I would have the frequency of this station over in Britain that would be sending any information that we might need. For instance, we might need a diversion when we came back because the weather would close in on the drome and they would send you somewhere else.

Every half-hour broadcast you got sent one number. You had to write this in your logbook and that was to prove you had been listening out – like, say, it would send out '5'. On the half-hour I always had to be listening and I had to have every number written in my book when I came back. If there was anything like a diversion, it would be sent out in code, in groups of four letters. Every trip you had a code book and for every operation the code book was different. Every two letters would be a phrase, and if it was such that it couldn't be phrased it would be sent out as plain language with two letters for one letter. You would write it out and find out what was said. That happened on every trip.

The actual station, when it was sending out its messages, sent them about 10 or 12 words a minute, very slow, and it sounded like this when it came over: 'daa daa de daa de daa de daa...' It was so loud you couldn't miss it and you knew what frequency it was on. That way you could make sure you always got information to the crew, whatever it might be.

The transmitter that was sending out was the biggest one in Britain, at Droitwich. There was a big, terrific mask there and the Germans used to try and block all your broadcasting because we had 'Gee', the code name for this apparatus we had. You could navigate by it but unfortunately it never got you further than the coast. It was a screen and the navigator had it on his table. I had to work it as well in case something happened. It was like blips on a screen and you could navigate by it but, when you got to the enemy coast, 'grass' started to come up the screen and they blotted it out with interference.

I think there were three stations then that were sending out a signal and receiving a signal back. As the signal bounced back to them, they could plot us as the enemy was approaching. That helped them to make sure they put the Spitfires and the Lancasters where they were needed – fighting the enemy.

I would always have headphones on. We all had them on because we had intercom – intercommunication – between each member. Before we took off the pilot would always check on every position to make sure everybody's radio, the intercom and headphones were working.

You never used personal names when you were in the aircraft and flying on ops. It was always very strict – strict and disciplined – so that we were at maximum efficiency.

Generally, we never saw anything until we got to the target; we were very fortunate in that respect. But once we reached the Ruhr, on our first trip, what a sight it was. Going over the target you could see the fires burning where those before you had dropped their bombs – the buildings were burning. The ack-ack was coming up together with both light and heavy flak. Some of it had got tracer in and you could see this flashing past you like rain going the wrong way past the aircraft.

When we started the pathfinders were just beginning. They would drop what we would call the green and red TIs (target indicators). They were like cascades of light dropping in green and red, and the idea was to bomb the reds or, if there were only green ones, you bombed the middle of those when you got immediately to the target.

As you approached the target you would get onto the heading you had been briefed to be on. You might be on a heading of 016, then when you were coming back you would be more or less on the reverse route, doing a slight circuit round the town and doubling back on yourself. As you approached the target the captain would say 'Bomb doors open' and that was the absolute worst part of the trip because then you were flying straight and level, which you had to do to give the bomb aimer a chance. His bombing sight was a marvellous and sophisticated set-up called a Mark 20. He would then guide the pilot into the target saying, 'Left a bit, right, steady…' This could go on for about 20 to 30 seconds but it seemed a hell of a long time when they were throwing all that muck up at you. The old joke was that you wanted to say 'Left, left, right, right, steady, back a bit,' but of course you couldn't do that.

When the bomb aimer said 'Bombs gone' you would feel the lurch of the aircraft as the bombs went. It would shoot up 200-300 feet. You lost so much weight from the bombs that the plane would just 'jump up'. Then the bomb doors would be closed and we would get the hell out of there.

We then had to make our way back. The most annoying thing about it was that going to the target you almost always had a tail wind but coming back you had a head wind. That was the prevailing wind from Britain to Germany, and of course with the head wind it would take you twice as long. This seemed a hell of a long time when you knew you were over hostile country, and if you just slid over a bit you were over the area that was heavily defended. On the way back you often saw a load of flak on one side and you knew that you had strayed, the navigator had got it wrong and you went sailing over a main target. Many times an aircraft would get shot down simply because it had wandered off track.

Before we even crossed the coast into Germany, or wherever we crossed the enemy coast, we always did what we called weaving. If you thought there was any danger of fighters about or even if there was flak or searchlights, you would do a corkscrew, maybe a gentle one, sometimes a violent one. You would put your nose down port, then go up starboard, then level off. You were constantly going in this method to the target and the only time you were straight and level was when you dropped your bombs. On the way back it was the same thing, corkscrew all the way back. It made you feel a bit sick sometimes and your nerves were in a bit of a state, particularly when you looked out and saw what a mess it was … and you could see the planes bombing under you.

Occasionally you would see a plane below going over the target and you would see a fighter coming up behind it. You wanted to shout out to warn them. 'Look what's coming! Watch out! Can't you see him?' I've seen it where the fighter came very close and the gunners didn't see him. Sometimes he came from underneath and they didn't see him until it was too late. Also, I've seen them rake straight across the aircraft, then a few seconds later there would be a hell of an explosion and all that was left was a big black puff of smoke. That could have been a Lancaster, a Halifax, a Wellington or a Stirling – then there's nothing. No crew – seven men gone – just a puff of smoke in the sky. I saw that on various occasions.

Sometimes you would see one go past and you could see very plainly that it was a Lancaster with all the camouflage colours. It was as clear as daylight, but as it was diving down the back half of the plane would be a mass of flames. He had either been shot at by a fighter or hit by flak, which would set the bomb bay alight, or maybe a wing or an engine, and there was nothing you could do about it except watch as he went slowly out of sight. You just hoped that some of the crew would get out. Sometimes a gunner and a radio operator would get out, or maybe even four or five of the crew, but it rarely happened that many got out when they were in that position. You could be the best crew breathing, but if ack-ack hit you there was damn all you could do about it.

Eventually you would cross the coast with a sigh of relief. The aircraft would start to come down and increase speed as we crossed the North Sea. As you hit the coast you would have IFF (identification friend and foe), which I had to work. This would be switched on and it told the defences in Britain that we were a friendly aircraft. It was a special coded signal that was sent out from a box at the side of me, preventing us from being confused with enemy aircraft coming in to bomb Britain. You would then make it back to your own aerodrome, which was amazing because they had to put the lights on round the dromes for you to come in to land. There were so many airfields across Lincolnshire, Nottinghamshire, Norfolk and Yorkshire with the outer perimeter lights well off the dromes themselves, and they all sort of overlapped each other. It was funny how often one would land at the wrong aerodrome. You had occults and pundits that would light up a code and you knew the code for your own camp. On one occasion we came back from ops and landed, and I thought, it looks a bit odd, this. It turned out that we had been given permission to land and we landed at the wrong drome. We took off again sharpish and got back to our own drome. This happened occasionally because there were so many airfields for Bomber Command, all down the east coast from top to bottom, that overlapped.

On landing, which was a relief, you got out of the aircraft, lit a cigarette and waited for the transport to come out for you. We'd get into a coach or wagon and head back to HQ to the briefing rooms. The first thing you did was go and get a brew, then sit down at a table. The majority of us smoked, so we'd have a cup of tea and a cigarette.

Before we could go anywhere we had to be debriefed by the intelligence officer. We would tell him if there was anything unusual on the raids, if we'd seen any fighters, where we'd seen them, etc. If we'd seen any of ours shot down they asked if we could tell them the number or the letter on the aircraft. They asked us what we thought of the raid, where we dropped the bombs, if we thought we were on target, and so on.

We then made it back to the cook house for our flying breakfast. We got an egg, which then was really something – you only ever got an egg if you were flying on ops. A proper egg and bacon breakfast was one of the perks of flying on operations. It was then a case of back to bed, keyed up but very happy with yourself, especially when you were walking back to your billet early in the morning. The fields were fresh, the sun would be just coming up and you would walk along a country lane thinking the world felt wonderful because you had got through the night, a very tense and stressful situation. As you walked back you felt at peace with the world and the grass seemed a lot greener.

3. Among the best

The next day was a rest day and the day after that we were on operations over Düsseldorf, another Ruhr town. We went through the whole procedure again as we had for Dortmund, with the briefing, the air tests, the meal, then setting off. This was 25 May, which was followed by a day of rest, and the day after that was another operation, at Essen. Another day of rest, then on ops again at Wuppertal, which even though it was the peak period of RAF bombing over Germany was still pretty fair going when you were bombed every other day, four times in around six days more or less.

When Essen came up we had heard about the place. This was the home of the munitions manufacturer, Krupp, and it was really heavily defended. Of course, all the targets were heavily defended, but Essen was really something. I remember going in to briefing for this raid; it was a period when every target was more or less to the Ruhr. At that time of the year it was during the period of the shortest nights and, as we bombed at night to help defend us against fighters in particular, it was a short trip. We were tied to the Ruhr because that was where we could do most damage over the industrial towns and help to spoil their war effort. We had heard all about Essen from crews who had been before. They showed us the map and we would see it was the Ruhr. Then we were told by the wing commander, 'Well, tonight's target is Essen…'

As soon as the wing commander said that, the atmosphere in the room changed – you could have cut it with a knife. Everyone knew its reputation. You could see the gaunt look on their faces, the white faces. You knew that when you went to Essen, the defences would throw everything bar the kitchen stove at you. This was our third trip; we had already done Düsseldorf and Dortmund and come through without a scratch.

The flight to the target was pretty much as it had been previously – across the coast, gaining height – and as soon as we got to the Ruhr we could see the flak and the flares and the searchlights going up over Essen. What an unbelievable sight! All the other targets were heavily defended, but Essen was something else. The Krupp's factories had anti-aircraft defences second to none. They were making every effort to save their works and the heavy flak was amazing. As you approached to do your bombing run straight and level, it made you wonder how the hell you could get through there in one piece. I remember on this particular raid, in the distance I could see a blue, powerful searchlight. I had been told about this before. They just flashed on and were electronically controlled. They flashed straight on to the aircraft, and as soon as they got it in the beam of the blue light all the other white searchlights latched straight onto it. Unless the pilot moved really fast and put the plane into a steep dive and turn, losing at least 6,000 feet as fast as he could, he'd had it. On this occasion one pilot never got out of that blue searchlight.

As we were approaching, with all the other searchlights hitting him, he just looked like a moth in a light. All the ack-ack was being shot up to the searchlights and all the time he was losing height as the aircraft was damaged. Sometimes you would just see a flash and that would be it, but on this particular night this aircraft slowly lost height and the searchlights followed it all the way down until it hit the deck. He never had a hope in hell of getting out, having left it too late. Once you had all the searchlights on you it was just like being in broad daylight. You had no chance at all. Fortunately, we got through without a scratch and we got back to base. It was quite a revelation for us to see the targets so heavily defended.

Our fourth target was Wuppertal. Again we went to the Ruhr, during what was called the Battle of the Ruhr, which was quite true. Our first trip had been on 23-24 May, the next was the 25th-26th, the next the 27th-28th, and this one 29-30 May 1943. In seven days we did four operations – pretty good going at any time for Bomber Command. We got there and back without anything untoward happening, landing quite safely.

We then had a gap of almost a month before we flew on ops again. As the nights were short, and as we only flew at night for safety reasons to avoid the fighters, it meant we could only get to the Ruhr and back. We couldn't go to targets further afield and had to wait for the longer nights to come along. Also, after the raid to Wuppertal, the reason for the one-month break was what we called the 'moon period'. When the moon came up, it was as good as daylight almost – they could see us with no trouble at all. So most raids, except on a few occasions for various reasons, were done on moonless nights. Consequently you would have a rush of ops, then almost a month when you didn't fly on any operations. During that period, of course, you were doing all sorts of exercises. The bombers were doing bombing runs on a bombing range and various other exercises kept us up to scratch.

Our next run of ops was to Krefeld, Mülheim, Wuppertal and Gelsenkirchen – four trips in five nights. Now that was really moving. By the time you'd finished those four trips you were shattered and your nerves were taut. After the first trip they used to give us some caffeine tablets to help keep us awake at night, because doing two nights running you started to get drowsy. We were very fortunate with these four raids. Everything went according to plan.

Three days after that we went to Cologne for the first time. That was quite a bit further on than the Ruhr. We did three Cologne runs pretty close together, one at the end of June and the next two during early July. On one of these trips we had a code name for the type of bombing. If it was reasonably clear and the cloud didn't interfere with the target, that was called a 'Parramatta'; I believe it was named after mountains in New Zealand or Australia. If it was 10/10ths cloud, where you couldn't see the target at all, that was called a 'Wanganui'. This particular trip it was a 'Wanganui'. The way you bombed on those occasions was to rely on the pathfinders. They would go in on dead reckoning by their navigator and also had extra equipment, such as H2S, which helped them to find the target and identify it through cloud. So we would go in and bomb on red target indicators, which, together with green indicators, would cascade down and the idea was to get the middle of the red markers if you could. We got through this raid with no particularly bad incidents – there was flak although it was 10/10ths cloud.

5 Group had a system whereby every aircraft on Bomber Command that went over enemy territory carried a camera. We had a device that was timed to go off as the bombs landed, so when the bomb aimer pressed and the bomb doors opened, the camera would take a photo. Photoflash it was called, and it was 2 million candle power. You had to be absolutely on the centre, within half a mile of the bombing target, and when you got back to base the film was developed.

The day after a raid you would go down to intelligence and look at your photographs, which would all be up on a wall. They would be about 7 inches square in size and would have your name on, the direction you were flying, the weight of bombs, squadron, and all sorts of information.

Right A commemoration of the bombing raid over Cologne on 3/4 July 1943. Such photographs, with the names of the crew, were presented to those who had dropped their bombs within half a mile of the centre of the target. It is signed by the Honourable Ralph Cochrane, who was at that time AOC No 5 (Bomber) Group.

Below The 'aiming point photograph' given to the crew after the successful raid on Cologne on 28/29 June 1943. There is cloud beneath the aircraft, but out of it is emerging a great plume of black smoke, which was identified as a large oil refinery, proving that the bombs had dropped in the right place at the right time.

Nine times out of ten they were generally black with white wavy streaks across them, given the amount of flak and searchlights and burning fires. There was nothing you could see to get what we called an aiming point photo. Very occasionally, though, the intelligence people who checked these photographs would find something that would identify the area – a river, say – and if they could prove that your bombs dropped within half a mile of the centre of the target you got a photograph or a drawing of a Lancaster with all the names of the crew that flew that night. It would be signed by the air officer commanding flight group, Air Vice-Marshal the Honourable Ralph Cochrane. He was well known and very popular with all the crews in 5 Group because he used to go out of his way to visit so many squadrons every night when they were taking off on operations. He would visit the crews individually when they were out at their aircraft, and was a very charming man. Whether this applied only to 5 Group I don't know, but during our tour we got four of these aiming point photographs, which was a remarkable number really. Not because people hadn't bombed their targets, but because the photographs couldn't usually prove that they had as it was so unclear.

This particular time we went back after the Cologne raid. We looked at our photograph and realised we were going to get an aiming point photograph, and I thought, how the hell can you get an aiming point photograph when it was 10/10ths cloud? But you were highly delighted if you got one because they were so few and far between. It was a nice appreciation of what you had done. I don't know whether all the stations did it – I can only speak for 5 Group, which was my group, which we felt was the top group in Bomber Command. Maybe all the other groups felt the same, but we had the Dambusters in our group and they were always the ones called into any really major raids, so we must have been among the best. If you got one you felt you had achieved something.

On this photograph, which I still have today even though it is a bit wrinkled now, you can see that it is cloud underneath the aircraft, but out of the cloud comes a great plume of black smoke. This was identified by intelligence as being a large oil refinery in Cologne, and it proved that our bombs had dropped in the right place at the right time. That was one aiming point photograph that I think was possibly unique in the fact that we got it in 10/10ths cloud.

Our next trip was to Gelsenkirchen again, back on the old 'milk run' to the Ruhr. Then the next was a remarkable trip, in that it wasn't to a German target – it was in the middle of July and it was to Turin in northern Italy. In all the time I had been bombing there had been no trips to Italy – this was one of the first. It was 12 July and, at more than 10 hours, it turned out to be one of the longest trips that Bomber Command did. We bombed the target without much trouble, though I do remember one incident. As with the blue searchlights at Essen, this happened to us over Turin. We were going along, just getting ready to go onto a bombing run, when this searchlight came straight onto us. We lost height rapidly, diving about 6,000 feet. I had earache for a couple of days after because of the air pressure due to the steep dive. We had been told – and some reckoned that it worked – that by switching on and off the 'identification friend and foe' box, which we were supposed to switch on when we were approaching the coast going back, it turned off the spotlight. In this case, this is just what happened – I switched it on and off and the light went out. Whether it was my IFF or not, or whether the enemy was just frightened when he saw a Lancaster in his searchlight, I don't know, but the light went out. There was nothing else unusual about the bombing run. Once we left the target, that was when the trouble started.

We were briefed to fly more or less directly across France to Italy to bomb Turin, then our flight plan for coming back was to head straight back for the French coast on the Mediterranean. We flew along the coast as we were supposed to, straight to the Pyrenees in Spain. From there we were to cross the Bay of Biscay and over southern England back to base. That was easier said than done. As soon as we left Turin we hit terrific cloud. The Met had obviously boobed badly to send us because it was higher than we could go. You could often get cumulonimbus, which was treacherous cloud. It had been known to rip aircraft apart with the terrific winds and currents in those very heavy thunder clouds that go up to 30,000-plus feet. The highest we could fly was 22,000 feet. We set off back in this and couldn't get out of the cloud. I can see it now, that aircraft. They used to talk about having all the blue and green lights on your wings and propellers. Well, we had them all that night. They were all dancing along all down the aerials. I used to have a trailing aerial that I used to reel out, which was mainly on a medium frequency and was used for rescue or SOS messages if we were in trouble. It was used on medium wave for emergencies. I happened to touch it and I got a hell of a shock because the static electricity had just charged up on it, the way it was trailing outside. We were going through this all the way back.

We got over the Bay of Biscay and eventually came out of this cloud. I can remember it well now, thinking that we had all this drama while we were in the cloud, but once we were out of it we were coming back over England, which was unusual because, being a 10-hour trip, we were crossing the coast of Britain over Torbay and it was broad daylight. It was something like 9.00 or 10.00am. We were usually coming back at dawn, sometimes in the dark or just at first light. So we came up the middle of England with the sun shining on a beautiful day. I put the BBC on for the lads and we listened to the radio. We got back to the camp and landed, thinking what a great trip. We'd done 10 hours and got back safely. We'd done what we had to, gone through the horrible conditions and got back in one piece.

Coming away from the flights, we had just signed off feeling at peace with the world and everyone. We put all our equipment away and were just walking up the road from the flight when we looked up to see a Lancaster coming in to land. After 800 feet the pilot put his full flap on, coming round to go on his final approach to the runway, and I couldn't believe it. Right in front of my eyes, all the rear end of the aeroplane fell off and the plane went diving in just past the drome, into a field opposite the main entrance to the camp. It was a very, very sobering and sorrowful moment for all of us – this particular crew were friends of ours. The pilot was an Australian called Chapman, and he had five Scotsmen and a lad who came from not far away from where I live. He was called Jack Greenwood, the flight engineer.

Two or three days after, myself and my crew were at a service for this crew on the camp at the little church there, and I assisted in putting six of them on the train to send them back to their families. It was a very tragic time. They had obviously been through all this static electricity all through France. A number of the crews returning from Turin had been pulled well off their normal course and the navigators hadn't realised it; the gyros and compasses were pulled off course with the static electricity affecting them. Instead of making for the Pyrenees and coming over the Bay of Biscay, they had been drawn more inside, had gone over the middle of France and ended up coming up over the Channel. They would have been losing height over the Channel ports and were more or less a dead duck, for the defences round the Channel ports, where the submarine pens were, were horrendous, a bit like Essen. I think quite a number were shot down there. After almost 10 hours of a trip through bad weather, they were pulled off course. A tremendous number were lost through this. Some of those who managed to return backtracked the log of their navigator, proving that these planes had come back over the Channel ports instead of over the Bay of Biscay, and it was all down to very bad weather.

A couple of days later, out of the blue, we were sent down to stores and we were all issued with a tropical kit – khaki shirt, shorts, one of those tropical helmet type things. We thought it was hilarious and wondered what it was all about. Also, if I'm not mistaken, I think they issued us with francs and we weren't allowed to take any sort of identification with us. We always used to leave it behind anyway, but we weren't allowed to take anything at all that might identify us on this trip. Well, we presumed it was a trip. There were only six crews, by the way, and by this time we had done a considerable number of trips, 13 or 14, making us at that particular time a very experienced crew. There were not many crews that got past five or six trips during the Battle of the Ruhr in the middle of 1943. If you look it up in any of the history books you will see that we were losing more aircraft than we ever did before or after, because the concentration was so heavy and so many raids were done in such a short time. We were losing crews at a tremendous rate.

After so many operations we were one of the top crews in the squadron. They picked six of the most experienced crews and we were going on some operations that were obviously going to be different from anything we had done before. So we were kitted out, got this foreign currency, and made our way down to the flights to see what this raid was all about. The date was 16-17 July, four days after the Turin raid. It went up on the board. It was a place called Cislago, a small town in Italy. Nobody had ever heard of it. The outcome was that it was one of the first times they had ever attempted to use the master bomber raid, whereby there was one person in charge of all the aircraft on that raid. He would go round and on the RT – that was the radio talking telephone – speak to every crew and tell them when to go in and bomb, etc. There were six going from our squadron, and six Lancasters from 207 Squadron at Langar. This was the squadron that was at Bottesford before our squadron went there. One of their number was to become squadron leader, or was to be the master bomber.

We went for a briefing and found out that we were going to bomb this target in Italy. When we had bombed it, with the weight of bombs and petrol we carried, there was no way we could get back to Blighty because of the distance. There had been one or two raids months before where some targets in Europe had been bombed and they had then gone across the Mediterranean to North Africa, to a place called Blida, about 40km from Algiers. At that time we had just invaded the south of Italy and Sicily, and our troops, together with the Americans, were, as Churchill said, 'attacking the underbelly of Europe'. So to assist the troops down there and to help to cut the enemy supplies, the idea was to bomb the transformers that supplied the electricity for the railway in Italy. I understood that all the railways in Italy were electrically run and consequently every so often they had these transformers supplying the power. This place in northern Italy must have been one of the large transformer areas, so the idea was to go in and attack it, then make our way across the Mediterranean Sea.

I remember the start of the trip when we were over France. This was one of the few times when we flew in moonlight; as there was only a small number of aircraft it was thought a reasonable risk to take. We flew individually to the rendezvous point, 6,000 feet over the Italian Alps. It was a wonderful sight, not being used to flying in moonlight, to see all the countryside: the lanes, rivers and canals going across France and how lovely it looked in summer. When we got level with the Alps, which you had to cross at a minimum of 18,000 feet, my navigator pointed out to me. 'Look there, Louis, Mont Blanc,' he said. On our port side as we went over at about 18,500 feet, almost level with us was Mont Blanc, looking very majestic in the moonlight on our port beam. It was a wonderful sight. Then, of course, we had to lose height rapidly over the other side of the Alps because it was only northern Italy where we were going to bomb.

We arrived at the rendezvous point to meet up with the commander who was going to be the master bomber, and we circled and circled and called out on the radio telephone, but were getting no answer. We must have circled for a good half-hour. You started to wonder if something was going to turn up to have a go at us.

'Try and get in touch with his radio operator,' the pilot said to me. Our radio telephony had gone U/S – one of the very few times that we ever needed it except for landing, and the RT goes U/S. So he suggested that I try and get in touch with his wireless operator on WT. We had been told at briefing that if we had any problems with the RT then the wireless ops had to get in touch with one another on WT. I'd been given this call sign – which was his call sign, I presume – and I bashed out to him, giving him 'K carry on', my call sign. Immediately a call sign came back, but it wasn't him. It was group headquarters in Grantham and the wireless op there, listening out, must have had the same call sign in use in Britain. Although I was only at 6,000 feet over the Alps, the wireless operator in Grantham came back strength five, top strength, to say carry on with the message. I just had to ignore him because it was all secret and he wouldn't know anything about it, but it proved that I was on the right frequency. The master bomber's wireless op obviously wasn't listening out because he had got in touch with all the others.

As time went on it became too late to attack Cislago. We were given two alternative targets: one was La Spezia, a big naval station of the

Italian Navy on the Mediterranean. It was probably the largest naval station they had, similar to Portsmouth or Plymouth in this country. So we went in and attacked. We got some sporadic ack-ack but we attacked La Spezia on our own, then came out setting course for North Africa. It was a long trip, probably getting on for 10 hours. As all raids were secret we didn't have any injections for going abroad. We were going across the Mediterranean, dawn broke and it became daylight, so we changed into our tropical kit. The trousers were like long shorts – they looked terrible – and we had the khaki shirts and the topi on. We looked like Fred Karno's!

We settled down and the navigator told the pilot that it was a very long sea leg – there were no landmarks that he could pinpoint. We hit the North African coast. If you look at that coast along Algeria and Tunisia, there is nothing between them – it is just a complete run of brown arid mountains with no sign of life. There was nothing on the maps that we could pinpoint our position with. So he said to the pilot, 'I think the best thing we can do here is turn to starboard until we see Algiers, then I'll know where we are.'

We did this and, of course, we were using up petrol in the meantime. It wasn't a tremendously long way to Algiers but we came back just a mile or two inside the coast flying in the direction of Blida. My navigator, as he did when we were on Coastal Command, started asking for QDMs – courses to steer – with me getting bearings. The bearings were hopeless. I got in touch with Blida on the WT and this operator was sending me courses to steer that I was passing on to my navigator. He was throwing them up in the air. I won't repeat what he was saying because it was the same as he had said over the Bay of Biscay. The navigator always said it was my fault, but I couldn't help that they were third-class bearings. As the hills were so high around us, the signals were just bouncing off, giving us no clues as to where Blida was. I had been bashing out for these QDMs when, suddenly, I put myself into the intercom. I could hear them discussing whether they should bail out or ditch over the sea because the engines were showing no petrol on the gauge. Suddenly the pilot said we were landing. 'We have found a little drome here,' he said. Not the one we wanted, and I'm looking out of my little window and hanging on.

'Hang on a minute,' I said. 'I haven't even got my parachute harness on.' I quickly grabbed the harness and parachute and put it on in case I needed it.

I could just see it out of the window. It was a grass drome, not very big. There were no runways, just grass. It was a French drome. The planes looked like they were from the last war. There were just one or two little biplanes round the edge and I wasn't too sure about it. The pilot was going to try to land. He made a circle and went in to land, and I said, 'Good show.'

'Shut up,' he said.

By the time he had touched the wheels down we had gone past the runway. I could see out of the little window that we were heading for a building and there were telegraph poles and wires going across. It was obvious that it was a railway station in a cutting and all we could see was the top. We were bouncing through a vineyard, so I was hanging on the pole at the side of my set looking out. After we bounced along through this vineyard we crossed the cutting and it took the undercart completely off. We left it behind on the railway line and landed, pancaked, in the next vineyard. When we had gone round on the circuit to try and land, the pilot had told the engineer to put the full flap on, but he couldn't move the lever at all. Whether that had been caused through heat or we had been damaged over La Spezia we don't know, but he couldn't get the flaps down. Consequently the air brakes didn't work and that was how we landed. Usually you land at around 85-95mph, but we touched down at 120mph, so this little drome had just shot by and we ended up in the vineyard.

We waited for the hiss and sizzle but nothing happened – it didn't set on fire – so we all got out as quickly as we could. I had to take all my coding books and crystals with me, so I was the last out. As I climbed out through the astrodome at the top, I got my backside burned because the aircraft was that hot from the sun. I had to smile. I remember the bomb aimer scuttling out before I could get out with all my tackle – there was him and the rear gunner who were both only small. The bomb aimer, Frankie Townsend, was shaking hands with this big Arab who had a big straw hat on his head. He was shaking hands with everyone saying 'Hello, hello', and we couldn't help but laugh. It was amazing how this bloke took it, because one minute he is tending his vineyard and the next minute he's got a dirty big Lancaster straight in the middle of it, and all he says is 'Hello, hello'. Anyway, the main thing was that we got out and before we could turn round there were hundreds of natives all around. I can't remember how we communicated with them because it was a bit out in the wilderness.

A French Army unit in the nearest village sent a Jeep out for us and took us back to the village. They treated us magnificently. They gave us a very good English breakfast and plied us with the local wine. In the officers' mess there were two French officers. I thought how scruffy they were, as neither had shaved for about three days, but they were very

Two 1940s postcard views of the city of Blida in Algeria. The city lies in the centre of a fertile district, and the cards depict the local and vegetable markets.

friendly and treated us like lords. They sent off to the drome and by the time they came for us, having had this breakfast and all the wine on empty stomachs, we were all a bit light-headed. Transport came to take us back to Blida, where we were debriefed and had to tell them all about the trip.

After we were debriefed we were told where we were going to stay while in Blida. The programme was that there were one or two of these shuttle raids where they were bombing somewhere in Europe or Italy, then going on to North Africa to Blida, this very big drome in the Middle East. There they would regroup and, eventually, all go back when the weather was right to bomb on the return flight. Of course, we had no aircraft.

They found us somewhere to stay and, as the children were off for the summer and we had palliasses, we were sleeping in a school house in the middle of Blida – right next to what I presume was a mosque. There seemed to be mainly Muslims there. This building had tremendous steps at the front. It was a very big place for the size of the town, with a large clock tower and bells that rang every 15 minutes day and night. On the half-hour and hour they rang for about a minute, and at the quarter-hour they did a ding-dong. This went on all night long, so you couldn't get much sleep. It was also very hot, which we weren't used to. We were wearing these shirts and shorts and a topi. We had to draw our stripes with a pen or pencil on our arms, but had no insignia of any description. We all had white legs when all around us had their khaki uniforms cut in style and were looking really smart and brown. They must have looked at us and thought, who are this lot? We looked anaemic compared to them. We were there for the best part of a week because the weather in England wasn't good enough for us to fly back.

In the meantime we met a crew who had been out on a shuttle raid, probably weeks before, one of the first I think. The pilot was called McIver, and they were sick to death with their situation but one of their engines was duff and couldn't be repaired. I don't know whether it had been shot with flak or what, but they only had three engines, so they couldn't go back until they got another. This was supposed to be being shipped out by sea, but at that time life for the Navy in the Mediterranean was horrendous. There were more ships being shot down between Malta and Gibraltar than Soft Mick because they had to go through the narrow straits near Malta. The Luftwaffe seemed to have absolute run of the place and there were very few getting through.

Eventually, they cannibalised our plane at the vineyard, taking a couple of engines off, one for them and one for another plane that was on the same flight as us, so they went back soon after that. We had no plane and were in dire trouble because they had been there months. There was a wing commander from Bardney, 9 Squadron, in our group. He arranged to bring us back together with several others and we were called sick personnel. Before that, my navigator had been commandeered to fly back with another crew.

After we had left Cislago to go to La Spezia, the others must have eventually arrived at this rendezvous and bombed the transformers. One of the planes from our squadron on this mission was followed round by a Junkers 88. It was shot up and the navigator was killed. We knew him – at the start of the trip he came out with us in the same transport that took us to our plane. The navigators were always a bit behind the rest of the crew because of all the various routes they had to map out. I always remember him, he was a very nice lad but he got killed. So our navigator flew with that crew back to the squadron.

Every day when we couldn't get back we went in the big army transport down to the nearest beach and spent part of the day swimming in the Mediterranean, which was very nice. It helped to pass the time and keep us occupied. We went down a major road along the coast and on the way back would pass all these native wagons, which were a bit rickety and not very high. They had a flat back and were piled high carrying boxes of grapes to the market. Our transport was much higher, so we were level with the top of the load. Regularly we'd lift one of these onto our wagon as we were passing, then sit eating grapes. The obvious thing to do was to squeeze them to get the middle out and not eat the skin because there were flies everywhere. They were also sprayed with all sorts of stuff, so you didn't eat the skin. My flight engineer, Bill, didn't think about this, and one day he just ate them whole. The day after he was a very sad and sorry man. He developed dysentery and, believe you me, it was really severe. Afterwards he told me that when he went to the toilet he immediately had to go back to the end of the queue again. This went on for about three days. He wasn't very big to start with, but he was going downhill fast because he was losing weight. Anyway, we had to go before they set off back on the bombing raid to Leghorn (Livorno). Just in time, Horry, the navigator, managed to go to the hospital and get Bill the engineer released. He got him on the same plane as himself to get back. We left Blida the day before they set off – myself, the two gunners, the pilot and the bomb aimer. We set off back as passengers with a wing commander from Bardney.

Our first leg was to Gibraltar. I have been to Gibraltar since and it really hasn't altered much as a drome. There was just one runway that ran past the rock, quite long. It was a bit like landing on an aircraft carrier – you had sea at both ends. The road across the border with Spain went through the Spanish customs, then straight across the middle of the runway to the other side. The traffic moved there into Gibraltar, so every time a plane came to land they had to hold up all the traffic and pedestrians until it had landed, then they could continue across the runway. We stayed there that night, so we went in the sergeants' mess for a drink. This was in a large Nissen hut, a sort of RAF pub with brick walls inside for corridors. We heard a siren and the barman said, 'You'd better stand in the lobby,' which was where the brick walls were.

'We're not bothered about that,' I said.

'Only they're blasting in the rock,' he said.

All inside the rock was like a labyrinth where they had all these guns pointed out over the straits and all the ammunition. It was a warren of passages inside the rock, which people can actually still go through today if they visit Gibraltar. He told us that they were blasting so we had better go in there. He went down on the floor and lifted a huge rock – it must have weighed about 20lb.

'It's only three or four days since this came through the roof,' he said.

So we didn't need asking again to go and stand in the corridor.

The following day we went out to the aircraft expecting to make our leg across the Bay of Biscay and back home. What I haven't mentioned is that before we left Blida we got in the aircraft and, of course, we were out there with just one rucksack more or less containing towels and soap, etc. While we were out there we were buying whatever we could in wine, all kinds of fruit and monkey nuts, which hadn't been seen in England for years because of the war effort. Only essential things were coming in and luxuries such as monkey nuts and oranges were very hard to find. We took what we could from Blida and filled our rucksacks before we got on the plane.

This wagon turned up, and was absolutely full. It had those carboys that you put acid in. They were full of wine – I don't know how many of them had been brought on board. They also had boxes of bottles of wine and champagne and all sorts of fruit. The wireless op and the navigator even had to have them under the tables and all down the fuselage. We had to lie on the boxes because there was no more room up front. There must have been up to 20 of us including the crew on this plane. The night we stayed in Gibraltar the wing commander had made some arrangement with the group captain – who was the commander at Gibraltar – that we could take bananas and other things we bought. We got our share, what we could carry ourselves, but he filled the rest of the aircraft up with all this stuff from the countryside. The next thing, from all over Gibraltar base, there were airmen coming with small parcels and the arrangement that had been made was that they would all be placed in the bomb aimer's compartment in front of the front turret. The nose of the Lancaster was filled with parcels. They were all being sent to England, then from the local post office in Bardney village all over the country. There were cameras, watches, jewellery, all sorts of stuff, but that, of course, was beating Customs. So taking all this fruit and alcohol had made the aircraft really full.

We set off the day after we had landed. We were well out in the Bay of Biscay, sitting there lounging back, trying to play cards to pass the hours, and suddenly the wing commander came down the aircraft smoking a cigar. He was the only pilot on board – we knew that – so he had just put in 'George' – the automatic pilot – and was having a stroll around the Lancaster. There he was smoking a big cigar, a bit like Churchill but taller. I wasn't too happy until he had got back in that seat. Eventually, though, we got back to Bardney and I can see it now. We got on the RT, and it took out two average-size lorries to collect all this stuff, which was obviously going to be used in the officers' mess. Whatever he had done, he had done a very good deal one way or another. No doubt they would be well up in their supplies in Bardney's officers' mess for quite some time to come.

4. HIT

When we got back it was the weekend and we were due for leave. So I left the following day and came home to live with my mother in Oldham. She had still kept the shop going during the war. It was a Sunday and I was knocking on the door but there was no answer. Then I suddenly realised it was my brother's birthday and he lived not that far away. In the lounge upstairs above his butcher's shop, all the family were celebrating his birthday. I landed with my wines and bananas and it made it more like a Christmas party. It was always good to see your family. We were always going out, my mother and all the family, making the most of it while we were at home.

After a short leave, the next trip was to Genoa, another Italian target. We must have hit the target as we got another aiming point photograph. Then we attacked Mannheim. Milan came next, followed by one of the major targets of the war – Peenemünde! This target was so important that it was considered a major factor in winning the war.

Peenemünde was an experimental station where they were building V2 bombs; these pilotless missiles that were far ahead of any bomb the war had yet produced. In fact, you could say it was the forerunner of the Shuttle!

Our spies found a way of letting us know how to bomb it. The only information we had was by way of a picture of this small headland in the Baltic with a small tower on it, and they knew that from that point to the target would take a Lancaster flying straight so many seconds. This was the only way they could tell us how to bomb; they had no pinpoint or knowledge of what was on the Baltic that they could use as a point to take as a heading to go and bomb Peenemünde. We were being trained but we didn't know what we were going to bomb or anything.

You had to be an experienced crew. We had done about 16, which made us experienced, because normally you did 30 on a tour. The idea was that from one point the navigator would set a course, would count so many seconds, then you would drop your bombs. There was no other way to recognise this trajectory off the coast, not far from Sweden. From there you would fly at 6,000 feet on the given heading for so many seconds, the pilot would steer the course and the bomb aimer would drop the bombs. Anyway, they didn't tell us until the day that it was Peenemünde, this secret place where they were making these bombs.

Somehow they smuggled this picture out, enlarged it as much as possible and reproduced it for every squadron. This was all we had to look at as it was projected onto a screen, with a little epidiascope, and it was the only intelligence we had before going to bomb. From our point of view it suddenly became rather remote because, after we had all the briefing and we got out to the aircraft, everybody was getting ready and running their engines up. We had already done the air test – as we always did in the morning – to make sure everything was shipshape.

The rear gunner got in his turret and the elevation and depression of his guns would not work. The hydraulics worked from one of the engines, the starboard outer, if I'm not mistaken, but somewhere along the line there was a problem. They were going to scrub us off operations but we had been practising for so long and it was something different so we really wanted to go on it. The pilot was doing all he could with the wingco and the flight commander to get them to give us a chance and let us go. He said that if we could fix it in a short time, we could make the time up on the first leg before we got to the target. Eventually they agreed to let us go and we were half an hour late setting off. But what the wingco or the flight commander hadn't realised was that where we would normally do a short cross-country to gain height, there was no cross-country because it was a long trip. So it was just one long sea leg right from our drome to the target and over the Baltic. We went a bit over Sweden as well to avoid the flak, then came in on this point, so we never made a minute up on time. Originally we should have been in the first wave because we were experienced. I think the raid was timed to last about 20-25 minutes and we were going in after everybody else had gone, more or less.

So we got to the Baltic and this business of going for this headland just didn't exist for us because we could see everything was on fire. It was a marvellous raid. All the waves that had gone in before us had done an excellent job. They had bombed every part of it, where the scientists and the workshops were – it was all ablaze. We were going in half an hour late and a lot of the smoke and cloud had blown away so we had a clear view.

We were detailed to bomb at 6,000 feet, which we did, and we had a great view of the target.

One thing we did see, though, was the number of aircraft shot down on the ground below burning. From that point of view, in terms of the losses, it was a very expensive raid. I believe we lost about 42 planes over the target that night. Normally there were diversionary raids that took the enemy fighters somewhere else long enough for us to get away. These planes, whether through their spies or whatever – I don't know – had got some knowledge of what was happening, and were waiting for the first wave going in; the majority of losses were from this first wave, which we should have been on. Being half an hour late turned out to be a godsend for us because by the time we arrived all the fighters had gone; they were running out of petrol and had to go and land. However, we had a very comfortable raid. We saw everything and went through, bombed our target and got out safely. I remember it now, going back to the flights and saying to someone who had landed before us, 'That was a good show. Great raid wasn't it?' and they told me where to go because they were all ashen-faced. It had been a real ordeal for those who had been earlier on the flight than us. You could say it was the luck of the draw – we came off lucky, because we lost two experienced crews on that trip. It was later said by Churchill and by Butch Harris, the commanding officer of Bomber Command, that that raid put the V2 bomb back six months and more than likely helped to win the war, probably as much as any air raid that took place at any time.

Five nights later our target was Leverkusen, back to our normal high-level bombing, which took place without incident. The night after that we went to the crew rooms to be briefed and somebody whispered, 'It's the big city,' which meant, of course, Berlin. That had everybody on their toes immediately. Berlin was renowned for being very heavily defended, similar to Essen only on a much bigger scale. They threw everything at you all right and, not only that, when you went to Berlin you were covering twice the distance as you were for the Ruhr, meaning the trip was more than 8 hours and you had 4 hours longer over enemy territory. We accomplished that without any untoward incidents, although we did see several fighters over the target silhouetted against the fires.

It was almost a month later when we flew again. In September we did two trips, both to Hanover, which were exceptionally successful raids. One was on the 22nd and the other on the 27th, and both were accomplished without any untoward incidents.

On 2 October we had a unique flight. Just delivered to the squadron was the very famous 'S for Sugar', which eventually did 137 trips over Germany, France and other enemy territory. Printed on the side was the famous statement made by Herr Göring that no enemy aircraft would cross the Rhine. That rather showed up his statement. We flew to Munich, one of the longest trips that 'S for Sugar' did. We also accomplished that with nothing untoward and got back quite safely. The 'S for Sugar' that we flew that night was the third trip after it had come to our squadron, already having done more than 80 trips with 83 Squadron before it was transferred to 467 Squadron. That aircraft is preserved in the museum at Hendon and the public can go and visit it today.

On 4 October the raid was to Frankfurt, which was quite a target and well defended. By this time my pilot had become a squadron leader, Squadron Leader Locke, a flight commander in 467 Squadron. Just before the raid, he came over to me. 'By the way, we're taking that plane that was stuck out in Blida when we were there,' he said.

This was the one whose crew had been stuck out there for weeks because they needed another engine and ended up taking one of the engines from our crashed plane. The plane had only just come back and had not had a proper service or anything.

'It's a bit dicey this,' I said. 'Look at the turrets.'

There was sand everywhere. It had been in the desert for a couple of months and sand doesn't do a lot for the hydraulics system.

Anyway, we were taking it. This was rather unusual in a way because the fitters hadn't had time to remove all the armour plating. Bomber Command had been directed by Commanding Officer Harris that only armaments that were immediately important, such as the armament behind the pilot's seat, were to stay, and that was the only one that was to remain. All behind his seat was just one big sheet right up above his head – one sheet of very thick armour plating, about a quarter of an inch to half an inch thick. Behind the main cabin, which I was nearest to, were these doors that shut the main cabin off from the rest of the fuselage. These two doors were very thick bullet-proof armour plating. The bullet-proof Perspex behind the engineer's head and also behind the engines was also armour plating. All this had to be removed to reduce weight so that the aircraft could go above the manufacturer's limit as to what we could carry. To do this they were taking all the armour plating off, leaving crews very vulnerable to fighter attack. However, the night we were taking this aircraft it still had the armour plating because they hadn't had time to remove it.

We took off for Frankfurt and that night, for the first time, we also carried new equipment called 'aural Monica', which was supposed to help us hear fighters approaching. It was connected directly to the intercom and I had to handle the equipment. It gave dashes and dots from each side of the aircraft; if anything was coming in from the port side, you would get 'dit dit dit' on the intercom, or from the starboard side a 'dat dat dat'. You had a small aerial under the rear gunner's turret transmitting a signal, and it was bouncing back to a receiver superimposed on the intercom. What we didn't know was that the Germans had this equipment and they were using it to come in on us. All we were doing was transmitting our position.

We approached the target doing the usual corkscrew to make it more difficult for possible fighters. Just as were levelling off to start the bombing run we heard this 'dit dit dit'. 'Turn that damn thing off,' the pilot said, because you couldn't be sure of it. It was the first time we had used it and we weren't really conversant with it. It was making this noise and the captain wanted to give instructions. It was getting on his nerves because it had been going on for quite a while, so I turned it off.

Only a matter of seconds after we turned it off I was in the astrodome looking out, which I always did if I wasn't taking the broadcast. The engineer was looking out of the bubble at his side, the bomb aimer was concentrating on the bombing run, and the gunners were looking out. As I was stood in the astrodome with one leg on the main spar and the other on my seat, something came from below on the starboard side, cutting across to go in high on the port side across the rear of the aircraft. There was a flash, flash, flash, bang – and I was on the floor. It was obvious I had been hit by something. The gunners fired at it, whatever it was. It raked us with cannon shells and then it went. This all happened in a matter of seconds.

I was on the floor. It took me a minute or two to get over the shock and it was like being hit with a big sledgehammer. I had been hit behind the knee of my left leg. I didn't know whether it was a bullet or what, but it hurt like hell. Up front there was more chaos because these shells had gone through; there was a smell of cordite, which you get with ammunition when it goes off, and there was smoke everywhere. There was confusion – nobody knew what damage had been done. The engineer mentioned that two engines might have been affected, but they kept running and seemed to be OK.

Of course, for a few minutes we were at sixes and sevens. We didn't know whether the engines would go or not, but it seemed as though the shells had missed, which was really lucky as the enemy came from behind. They had these up-shooting guns, so they were firing at you before you could see them.

When we had settled down and sorted it all out, we found that the engineer had been injured, but was very fortunate that he had this piece of bullet-proof Perspex behind him. It was right behind his head and had been hit right in the middle with a cannon shell, but amazingly it didn't affect his head in any way. Obviously, if it hadn't been there it would have taken his head off. He ended up with about 50 pieces of Perspex in his knee. It's amazing how it got to his knee from where it was – nobody knows how, but it did.

I too had been injured. I thought, well, they already knew that the engineer was injured and he does a fair bit with the pilot as far as engines and oils and magnetos, checking and so on. I didn't want the crew to think that the main communication man in an emergency was also injured, or they might start to panic. So I didn't say anything. I was a bit shaky and in a bit of a state, but I could still manage to do my job. We used to carry a dressing in our uniform. I had the same type of thing as this, only twice as big, in my drawer, so I ripped my pants and underpants, I got out this pad and tied it as tight as I could. There was blood all over the place, all over my hands and my logbook. I tied it tight round my leg and it seemed to stop the bleeding a bit, but it was rather numb and I was shaking.

Suddenly it was time for a broadcast. By this time the bomb aimer had said that all the incendiaries were on fire, so the pilot told him to jettison all the bombs, which was all you could do when you had incendiaries on fire. You only had a matter of minutes before the whole damn lot would go up. So he jettisoned the bombs and the navigator gave the pilot a course to steer, giving him a temporary heading until we could sort ourselves out. We were then on our way back.

I realised that, although I had criticised the pilot about the sand in the aircraft, it was a damn good job we had taken it that night because when we eventually did land back all the bullet-proof doors behind me were studded with cannon shells, which would have cut me in two and probably taken the engineer and possibly others as well! Luckily it missed the rear and mid upper gunner, splattered straight across all these doors, and also hit behind the Perspex. When they checked the aircraft when we got back, it had more than 20 cannon shell holes. The thing that had got me had gone round the edge of these on the skin of the aircraft and some part of a cannon shell had managed to ricochet around the corner, ending up in my leg. The aircraft that attacked us never came back. I don't whether our gunners damaged him or not.

We set off back with no air brakes. It had affected the hydraulics, which would also affect the flaps, and we didn't know what damage had been done to the body of the aircraft, the fuselage or the wings. The first thing I had to do was take the broadcast. We didn't often get any instructions from these broadcasts when we were flying on ops. Occasionally they might abandon ops or we might get a message, but very seldom did any instructions come through. We would just get the call sign and the number to take down so that the signal leaders knew that you had taken the broadcast by this number. This time they came over with a message. I wasn't really 100 per cent for taking messages, considering the state I was in, particularly the likes of this one. Messages never came over quickly, they were always very slow. It was Morse at about 8-12 words a minute. But it was a very powerful signal from Droitwich and it was 16 groups of four letters.

Every day you had a code book for any messages that came. You carried this code book and every day the code changed. There would be two letters that would mean course to steer, another two might mean weather not very good, and so on. So there would always be a phrase that was represented by two letters that were being transmitted to you in groups of four. Afterwards you got your book out and decoded it.

On this occasion the signal leader did it the hard way. I couldn't believe it when I decoded it because instead of using these two letters for each phrase, he was using two letters for one letter. At the end of the book was what we called plain language, and for every letter there were two letters of code, so if there were any words or phrases that you couldn't find in your code book you could work it out in plain language by using two letters for each letter you wanted to spell out. He did 16 groups of four to tell us that there was a weak weather front over Waddington. I could have screamed! It was the longest message that I ever took when I was flying on ops. The bloke who sent the message, the radio operator, if I could have got him I would have blasted him because I was not in great shape, especially as we were flying high, and low oxygen levels meant you tended to do things slower than you would on the ground. By the time I had decoded the message, with blood dripping on the logbook, I wasn't too pleased. Well, the pillock, I thought! It could have been done much more simply by three or four groups of four if he had looked the phrases up in the code book.

Anyway, I passed the message on to the pilot – the weather had deteriorated a bit. So we were on our way back, not sure of the state of the aircraft, and not knowing whether we could keep going and make it back to England, or whether we might crash before we got to the coast and ditch over the sea. No pressure then!

All the way back, as we got nearer the coast, I got on the emergency frequency. The highest degree of emergency is 'SOS', but I didn't think we were really that bad, so I was using the next emergency, 'O', which you transmit as 'da da da'. First of all, I would send the call sign to the station I was transmitting to, put my priority of distress, then relay our position, which my navigator was constantly giving me. Once we were over the sea I was sending it more often. Each time I would send 'O' and the position we were in, and press my key, and the direction-finder at each station would tune into my signal. They would get the strongest signal to get a bearing and where the three bearings crossed was where we should be. They followed us in that way all across the North Sea until we hit the English coast, then, of course, I warned them that we were over land and we could then get in touch by RT. Once we had cleared the North Sea, the biggest emergency was over. We now had the problem of wondering what the state of the aircraft was as far as landing was concerned. We had already had two instances of bringing the aircraft back from North Africa because we had crashed out there and they had used one of our engines to bring back. The next was that it had armour plating, which no other aircraft flying on Bomber Command had that night, so I think we were lucky to get back. The fact that it had come back from the Middle East and the armour plating was still there was lucky from our point of view. There was no question that it certainly saved my life.

Once we had cleared the sea and were over England, we got in touch with our own aerodrome. We explained what damage we thought we had and that Bill was injured. I didn't tell them until we were nearly at the drome that I was injured as well. They told us to divert to Wittering, where they had a 3-mile-long runway, as we had no air brakes and were shaky about the flaps. Then it came back to us again, which was another aspect of this raid – I have already said about the Turin raid, when those friends of ours, another crew, came all the way back from Turin in a similar state. They had probably been shot up, weakened at the rear of the fuselage, and when they put their flaps down they had crashed outside the main gate and were all killed. That was very much to the fore in our minds as we were making for Wittering. It was also one of the stations where they had petrol pipes that ran out, and they could light them, which helped you to land if there was fog. So we approached and everyone was insisting that whatever we do, we don't use any flaps. We would go in, get as low down on speed as we could and land with no air brakes, so the best of luck and here we go… We were certainly not going to put any flap down to try and slow us in case the stress on the rear of the fuselage would do the same as it did to Les Chapman and his crew.

We gradually came down as slowly as we could. Everybody was in crash position except the pilot and the engineer. The pilot made a good landing. Whereas we would normally land at around 85-90mph, we probably landed at around 110mph. We got down, felt the wheels touch, then we sat back and waited for the rumble as it went along. We slowly, slowly pulled the engines back and went the full length of the 3-mile runway, just running off the runway across the perimeter track and settling in the mud at the end. But there was no further damage and everyone was still in one piece. We then had the ambulance coming out and all the other various people coming to meet us. They came into the aircraft and I said, 'Oh, it'll be all right. I'll be fine in a couple of days'. They told me to get in the ambulance – I had no say in the matter. They had me on a stretcher and I was in. That was it, then. Bill, the engineer, and myself were whipped off in this ambulance and taken to Rutland & Stamford Royal Infirmary. It was only a small hospital, but we were treated like lords. We were in a hell of a state. They washed us and put us to bed. It felt great to lie in that bed and just relax.

The day after I wondered what was going on. We asked what was happening, as they seemed to be getting us ready for something. We were still in pyjamas. I couldn't wear the bottoms as my leg was too swollen, so I only had a pyjama top on. They told us that they were sorry but they couldn't keep us there. We were sorry too, because it was a lovely little spot. We were then on our way to an RAF base hospital, a damn big place just outside Sleaford, called Rauceby. In peacetime it had been a big mental hospital and I believe they just kept one ward with some of the long-standing patients in, with the rest of the hospital completely taken over by the RAF.

We landed there and they put us in the casualty ward. We were in there for a week or so, while we were at our worst. In total we were in hospital for six weeks, both with leg injuries, and strangely enough we were both ready for discharge at the same time. I could write a book about that six weeks in Rauceby Hospital. It's another aspect of being in the Air Force, completely different from anything else, and really in many ways it was quite an experience. Some of it was quite comical, some of it not.

At the end of the six weeks, Bill and I had to go for a medical before we were discharged. We had to wait outside this office where they were going to give us the necessary papers. I think we were going to get a fortnight's sick leave first. I was talking to Bill while we were waiting. He said that on one occasion he had been ill and on another he'd had to go home because his wife had been ill and she had a baby, and there were one or two other things. He had ended up being about four trips behind us – I think when we had done 20 he had done about 16 or 17.

Before he went in to see the doctors who were going to discharge us, I said, 'I tell you what you want to do, Bill. You know how you are with your eyes…' He used to have terrible eyestrain. When we came down after he had been looking out all night in the dark he used to have terrible strain on his eyes. We used to call him Popeye, his eyes used to be bulging out and bloodshot. '…You ought to swing it on your eyes and then you'll probably finish when we do.'

He went into the office after me. I'd already been in and been told, 'OK, you're on your way. A fortnight's sick leave, then back to your squadron.'

I was waiting for Bill to come out and when he did he said, 'I've got a note here. There's no way I'm going to get away without flying any more because of my eyes. They've given me a prescription for four pairs of glasses.'

Four pairs of glasses! That was one for day flying, one for night flying, one for reading and one for long distance. When you first joined up and you wanted to join air crew, anyone who had any defect with their eyes was out right away. They had no chance in air crew unless their eyes were more or less perfect. But once they've trained you and spent all that money on you, they won't waste you unless they have to. That was the end of Bill and me at Rauceby, and we were on our way to a fortnight's very welcome sick leave.

5. Testing Times

After the sick leave we were due back at the squadron, but while we had been in hospital there had been quite a change because my pilot had been promoted to acting squadron leader flight commander. The old 467 Squadron had been moved from Bottesford to Waddington, which was a big peacetime station with much better living accommodation, H blocks, etc, whereas Bottesford had been a war station with cold Nissen huts and dispersal camps. Now we were in the lap of luxury in the living quarters. We had bathrooms, drying cupboard, gymnasium and a lovely mess. We were like lords of the manor when we got there.

While they were transferring 467 Squadron over to Waddington, they took C Flight out of 467, of which my pilot was the flight commander, and we were the start of a new squadron, 463. To start with all there was of the squadron was just C Flight from 467, and my pilot was for the first week or two the acting squadron commander until a wing commander came along. We had to go and report back, and at this time the new wing commander for 463 arrived just before us. He came from a well-known family, Kingsford Smith.

Charles Kingsford Smith had been a famous pre-war flyer, one of the out-and-out pioneers of flying when they were flying from Australia to England, like Amy Johnson and Jim Morrison and all those at the start of the flying era. They were real heroes. They were flying in very poor single-engine aircraft all across the Pacific Ocean and the Atlantic Ocean in the early days of flying. Charles Kingsford Smith was unfortunately lost over the Andaman Sea near Burma. His engine may have packed in. He went in and was never heard of again, but he had set quite a few records in long-distance flying before this happened and had been a well-known figure at the start of the war. It was his nephew, Wing

Above Squadron Leader Harry Locke is second from left in this photograph. On the left is Wing Commander R. Kingsford Smith, squadron commander of 463 Squadron RAAF. To the right of Harry Locke are Flt Lt R. Mortimer, flight commander, and gunnery leader Flt Lt Brian C. Moorehead.

Below The memorial to Harry Locke in his native Australia. He died in 1999, aged 80.

Commander Rolla Kingsford Smith, who came to our squadron. He too was said to be a brilliant flyer.

So now I was back flying with my crew from Waddington, Royal Australian Air Force Squadron 463 instead of 467. My pilot was a flight commander, and I was back ready to fly again after my hospital stay and sick leave.

Fortunately, while I was away they had only done one operation and that was another to Berlin on 22-23 November 1943. I was very fortunate in that respect, because everyone who flew on Bomber Command and had their own crew didn't like having to fly with another crew. Obviously, if you missed a few trips you had to make them up by flying as a spare bod with somebody else. So Bill and I were back with our crew and our next operation with 463 Squadron was on 16-17 December, and lo and behold it was Berlin again. They called it a 'milk run', as at that time every other trip was to Berlin. This was our first trip after Frankfurt, which was quite an ordeal when you had been wounded. I can't say we were in the best of moods by any stretch of the imagination.

So we had this trip to Berlin and I think on this occasion we were routed in north of Berlin, more or less over the Baltic, then turning starboard and coming down from the north, bombing Berlin and coming back across Germany. As I remember it was quite a sight to see this from the last time we had bombed it, with the increase in the activity of the enemy by fighters and all sorts of gadgets. In fact, we could see these fighters, which were very active. There was bags of flak but the fighters were very active over the target.

I can see one now. It was when we had just finished bombing and I was looking out of the astrodome on our return journey. We were on the first wave and on our return, but still over Berlin. There were a tremendous lot of flights. A couple of thousand feet below was this aircraft. This fighter was closing up behind it. I wanted to shout, 'Look out!' It went straight up behind and it was unbelievable how close it was. There wasn't a thing I could do. Whether they didn't see him because he was underneath and coming up on them, I'm not sure. I was above so I couldn't really tell. Suddenly he sprayed the aircraft with cannon shells and the thing was on fire. Before you knew it, it just blew up and all that was left was black smoke. I remember that vividly.

Then on the way out, us having been on the first wave, the others were just getting to know the heading in and out over the target. Behind us I could see these flares. They were laying two lines of flares – it was just like coming out down the high street. These flares were hanging in

```
Air 27/1921

                                                          Time
Date     | Aircraft        | Duty                      | up   |down
         | Type & Number   |                           | 16.40 03.21
16/17.12   Lancaster III     Bombing- Berlin
           JA902

Crew S/L Locke H.B.
     Sgt Holt
     F/S Hassell H.
     F/S Townsend E.
     F/S Butler
     Sgt Brooks J.
     Sgt Munro T.
     F/S Lawson S.    2nd pilot

Details of Sortie or flight
Sortie completed. 10/10ths cloud. Red flares with green stars centre
of concentration of approx 6. 20,000ft. 20.02hrs. 1 x 4000HC. 950 x
4 and 100 x 4 XIB's. 48 x 30lb. Wanganui flares concentrated, but som
of green T/I's scattered. P.F.F. T/I's seemed to be very concentrate
There were no results of bombing observed owing to 10/10th's cloud.
P.F.F. were correct then it should have been a good raid. Firework
display over target, but not much flak. Route very good and navigat
excellent.

                                                                Time
```

Above A photograph of a page from the squadron Operations Book, giving an account of the 'milk run' bombing raid to Berlin on 16/17 December 1943.

Below The 'uneventful' trip to Brunswick, 14/15 January 1944.

```
                                                          Time
Date     | Aircraft        | Duty                      | up   |down
         | Type & Number   |                           | 16.39 20.21
14/15-1    Lancaster III     Bombing- Brunswick
           EE191

Crew S/L Locke H.B.
     Sgt Holt W.G.
     F/S Hassall H.
     F/S Townsend E.
     F/S Butler L.
     Sgt Brooks J.L.
     F/S Munro T.
     F/S Fairclough L.S.    2nd pilot

Details of Sortie or flight
Sortie completed. 9/10 cloud. Tops about 6/7,000ft. Centre of
concentration of 8 Wanganui flares. 21,000ft. 19.17hrs. 1 x 4000HC
1500 x 4 IB. 80 x 30. Glow of fires seen reflected on cloud as a
left target area. Target Wanganui flares fairly concentated and t
masy have been a satisfactory raid. The position markers were ve
scattered. Attack commenced about 10 mins. early. Spoof effectiv
fighter flares were laid Eastwards from Hanover and target area
fairly quiet. Route O.K. R/G displayed great initiative in firin
and frightening enemy a/c which was about to attack another Lan
```

the air and they were very, very bright. It lit up the whole area and it meant that all the aircraft coming out from then on were going to have to fly along this lane as though it were broad daylight. They were replacing them as they were going out. They had got the track of the aircraft going in and coming out and were laying a line of flares, so that every aircraft had to pass through it feeling absolutely naked. It had been mentioned by one or two people – and I actually saw this myself – that they had developed rockets that some of the fighters could fire and they were directional like you see today and are quite commonplace. As we were coming through this lit-up area there was a rocket a long way off but it was following us as we were corkscrewing. It sort of fizzled out, but it was definitely a rocket that had latched on to us in some shape or form and was coming along our path. However, it was well back and never really got close to us, but I do remember watching it. As we changed direction it changed with us.

We cleared the target and we were very fortunate. There was nothing untoward and everything went according to plan. We dropped our bombs and it looked to be a great success. There were fires everywhere, flares, TI markers, searchlights, fighters, the lot – like Essen, but two or three times bigger covering a much wider area. We were on our way back when probably the most traumatic event took place.

We had been routed just past Frankfurt, of all places, like the last trip we had done. I can remember standing in the astrodome looking out as we went past. We were on the outskirts, not directly over it by any means, but near to it and conscious of it. Standing in the astrodome looking out, my leg that had been injured suddenly started to quiver. It was dithering and I couldn't stop it. I suppose it was nerves, a reaction from the last raid on Frankfurt. This went on for about 15 minutes until we were well clear of the place, then it settled down again. My leg had given me a reminder of the near 'do' we'd had. Anyway, we returned and landed quite safely. Another successful trip.

Our next trip was on 14 January 1944, to Brunswick. On this occasion we had quite an uneventful trip. Everything went according to plan and we did our usual run in and bombed, and came away with nothing untoward happening.

Between the Berlin trip and Brunswick a month had gone by, and during that period we had only done two ops – the fact that my pilot was now the main flight commander in 463 was the main reason. He was only allowed to fly on operations when Group told him he could; he couldn't fly on operations without their permission. Over all the years of Bomber Command, the mainstays of this station – the squadron commander and flight commanders and their signals, navigation leaders, gunnery leaders, all these people – were only allowed to fly when Group command said they could, because they were hard to replace due to their experience. They were made to spin out their operations so that they had good command over each squadron. So this was happening with my pilot, and that's why we had only done two operations in a month.

After the Brunswick trip we seemed to go quite a while with nothing happening as far as ops were concerned. Harry Locke, my pilot, was running the flights and he had a lot of commitments, running the squadron, running the flight, the administration, etc, so we were in a way at a loose end. I used to cop out because, being a wireless operator, it was the old story – everywhere you were and whatever you were flying they were always grabbing the wireless op because no bomber aircraft could take off with just a pilot.

Waddington was a base station serving several squadrons in that area. It was responsible for all the Lancasters that were always coming in for replacements from the manufacturers. It was one of the base stations that accepted these Lancasters, and when they came to the squadron they had to be tested, given a thorough test flight to make sure that they were up to standard and there were no faults.

There was one squadron leader, whose name I cannot remember, who was resting from ops and had been sent to Waddington. He didn't have any kind of administration job but they had made him into a test pilot to test all the Lancasters that came in before they were distributed to the various squadrons who came under Waddington base. Consequently, they had to have a wireless op for these flights and I got called for this job several times. I don't know which was worse, going on ops or a test flight. On the test flight you would get the Lancaster with this squadron leader in charge. It would have a full load of bombs, full petrol, full weight, as if taking off for an operation. The only difference was that the bombs were not fused – they were there for weight purposes only. You would get to the end of the runway and he would send everybody into the tail. Normally when you were on ops in a Lancaster everyone came forward for the take-off. The two gunners would come and sit behind the doors right up near the main cabin, completely clear of the bottom so that you soon got your tail up. On these test flights they did everything in reverse. They did it the hard way to make sure that it was a really severe test for the aircraft. The pilot and the AID (Air Inspection Department) man, who was a civilian, would between them be responsible for accepting this aircraft into the RAF.

On a test flight you would also have a flight mechanic, a radio mechanic, armourer, and all the various trades of the ground staff. Each and every one had to be on board to check the equipment while they were airborne. They had to fly with the aircraft even though they were ground crew. You would fly for around 2 or 2½ hours and it was very monotonous, flying at around 22,000 feet going along steady, doing all sorts of turns and banks and checking all the equipment to make sure it was airworthy.

I remember one test flight in particular. We were going along nice and steady. When they got up to 22,000 feet they stalled the aircraft, put the flap down and let the speed fall off until we were going about 85mph. The aircraft would kind of yaw and suddenly the nose would drop, go into a stall and go down. What usually happened would be that the pilot would push the stick forward and let it go into a steep dive until his speed had picked up to around 110 or 120mph. He would then put full power on his engines, pull the stick back and pull out, getting back onto a normal course at a normal speed with flap up and flying straight and level again. You then knew that the framework and the strength of the plane were OK because of the stress that the stall would put on the aircraft.

On this occasion the AID man let the pilot get partially into the stall then said, 'Pull the stick back, pull the stick back.'

He pulled it back, only halfway into a stall, and lost speed when all you normally wanted to do was to pick up speed to get out of the stall and get back on course. The aircraft then started bucking like a bronco. My set was on rubber mounts to allow for the movement of the aircraft, and it was bouncing up and down like a balloon. I was jogging backwards and forwards and everyone else was doing the same. It was just as though it was going to shake everything out of the aircraft, the engines, the wings, the lot. Eventually the pilot put the nose down and pulled out of the stall. You should have heard the language. He turned on the AID bloke and said, 'Look, don't ever ask me to do that again,' and called him all the names under the sun. It was stupid. The stress and strain on that aircraft could have pulled the engines out. What he had in mind God only knows, but it wasn't a very comfortable half-hour while all this was going on. But we landed safely and everything was OK.

On another occasion on one of these test flights with this squadron leader we were coming in to land at Waddington and it was early evening, quite pleasant. On this occasion there was just the pilot and myself flying. I can't remember why, but it was some sort of air test acceptance and the AID was not present, nor were any ground staff. We were approaching the aerodrome diagonally and on one side we could see all the planes in the dispersal surrounding by the crews and equipment waiting for the word to go. On one side of the drome was 467 Squadron and on the other was 463 Squadron, probably with about 30-40 aircraft ready to take off when they got the signal from the flight control caravan. I don't know whether the pilot had decided that he wanted to opt out of this job and get a fresh posting of some sort, but he certainly made a damn good effort towards doing it because suddenly he just dropped it down on one wing and went straight across the drome, flying with one wing low, practically touching the deck. He was nearly cutting a groove as we went across. We then pulled up and flew over the top of the corner of the two hangars in the far corner, zoomed up, went round, then made our normal approach and landed. I thought, dearie me, how sad. I knew what was going to happen.

We eventually pulled up outside the hangar that we had flown over just moments earlier. I was very quick to get my parachute and harness and move off. I decided to walk very smartly up the flights to get out of sight as quickly as possible. 'Cheerio,' I said and I was off; I knew what would happen. I hadn't gone more than 100 yards when I saw three cars coming down like a funeral procession. In one was the group commander, in the next was the station commander and the wing commander, all three of them. Waddington, being a base station, had an Air Commodore, which was above the rank of station commander, a group captain, the squadron commander being a wing commander, and those three formed a procession in the cars to see this squadron leader as he got out of his aircraft. I didn't hear of the outcome but I don't think I ever saw him again. It wasn't surprising because if for any reason he had misjudged in any way, he could have blown up in the middle of the aerodrome. That would have been curtains for the 30 or 40 aircraft waiting to take off on operations that night.

It was about this time, after the Brunswick raid in January, when I was doing all this air testing type of flying – short flights up and down and here and there – that we were suddenly told that, while we should still have had two or three operations to do, we had finished our tour. At that period, after the heavy stuff we'd had all through 1943, I can't say that we didn't appreciate it. They decided that they couldn't afford to lose any more of the very experienced crews. There had been a lot of crews lost doing their last couple of ops, so the powers-that-be decided we had finished our tour! We had the 'big piss-up', then it was the parting of the ways. We had been together from October 1942 till April 1944, a very long time to fly together in the Air Force. It was like splitting up a family! It had got to March and we had finished the tour; between then and April I was posted away.

After leaving Waddington I was posted to Silverstone where they now have all the Formula 1 racing. I was posted there on flying duties as an instructor flying with pupil crews together with a staff pilot, staff pilot operator, etc. I was there for quite a few months. It was rather hectic because these aircraft weren't always 100 per cent – they weren't up to the standard of the squadron Wellingtons that were still flying on ops. The majority were what you called Wellington 1Cs, some of the early ones, so they were a bit dicey at times. I do remember while flying at Silverstone that we had what they call a flying pool. Myself and probably another nine or ten who had been on ops were just flying whenever they needed a wireless operator. This happened quite a few times.

They had a special course going on at Silverstone called a Group Efficiency Flying Course for Pilots, and they were flying these Wellington 1Cs, just taking off and landing and various other stuff. I didn't feel very happy about what they were doing; they were just going round on one engine and coming in to land. Then they would say 'overshoot' – full flap with only one engine. It was only a two-engine aircraft and there was a strain as it went over. You would have your fingers crossed and be praying, because the strain on that aircraft overshooting at full flap was tremendous. The slightest thing and it would all go up. That made you think that it would be a damn sight easier going back over Essen.

After a few months there I got a posting to a place called Husbands Bosworth, not far from Market Harborough and near where the Battle of Bosworth took place. This was a new OTU that had been put together very quickly, drawing staff members from all parts of the Group. It was amazing, and I really enjoyed every minute. Everybody seemed to be of the same nature, very friendly, and we all got on well together. It was a very happy camp. I was still instructing, and I remember on one occasion I had a full course of Canadian wireless operators. It wasn't too easy because you nearly had to teach them elementary maths to begin with before you even got started to think about the radios. Anyway, it was a very pleasant time. I was doing more work on the ground although I did quite a bit of flying. Suddenly they decided that it was getting to the stage after the second front that they were going to close the station down because they didn't need it any longer, and I was posted back to Silverstone.

By this time I had been promoted to a warrant officer and it was rather a cushy number in a way. I spent most of my time as warrant officer in charge of flying control signals, which sounds very important. It was looking after all the aircraft that were flying and I had a team of ground wireless operators to look after, keeping in touch with all the trainee aircraft that were going out on training flights both day and night. There were three of us and we worked round in shifts. It was quite a nice job.

There was one other incident that happened at Silverstone the second time I was there. I was going up from the mess one morning to the flights. As I went in there were Yank soldiers everywhere. One bloke was asleep on the pool table. 'What's going on here?' I thought. By the time I got up to the flights I had realised what it was.

I looked out on the drome and there were more than 50 Dakotas parked all over the dispersal. I had seen them at night; it happened quite regularly, these Dakotas flying at night in blocks of up to 50 aircraft, a hell of a lot. They all had their navigation lights on and they were flying in formation. Each one was full of airborne troops and they were getting ready for landing when the second front started. They would be some of the first troops to go.

On this particular night they had been flying and the weather had turned bad, so they had to land where they could. The drome where they were stationed had been closed down by bad weather and they had been ordered to land at Silverstone. Consequently they had all just found anywhere they could to get some sleep for a few hours until daylight. When I got up to the flights these Dakotas were already starting to go round the perimeter track to take off, which was amazing to watch. They went to the end of the runway one after the other, nose to tail, and they took off in the same way, with only yards between each aircraft. They got down to about the last six or seven when this American soldier came around the corner looking a bit bleary-eyed, not knowing where he was. Somebody threw a bike at him and said, 'There you are. You'd better catch one of them.'

There he was, bouncing along the runway on this bicycle to try and catch the last Dakota before it took off. Actually the last one was just moving off, and it had just released the brakes when this guy caught up with it, the doors opened and three or four of them yanked him in. It was really strange – we were all cheering him on. It was hilarious to see it happen, him chasing around the runway to catch the plane.

Eventually it came my time to be demobbed and I went to a place called Desborough, from where I was posted to Uxbridge, got my civvy uniform and came out of the Air Force at Christmas 1945. That was the end of my flying career in the RAF.

6. THE LUCK OF THE DRAW

On my return I went back to how things had been before the war, back to run the butcher's business. My mother, who had kept the business going all through the war, was glad for me to take the shop over, which I did, and eventually bought another shop. I enjoyed it – it was a very happy trade. By the end of my career, however, the media would almost have you think we were trying to sell poison. The vast majority of butchers' shops have now gone.

There were a couple of things that I haven't mentioned previously, the first being that the outcome of the trip to Frankfurt was that the pilot got the DFC and the engineer and I got the DFM. We were very proud to receive these honours, but another thing that I really appreciated was something that I didn't know until my crew came to visit Bill and me when we were in hospital. They had got together some transport to come and visit. They told me that in the station headquarters wireless signal room, which is quite a big room, they had written on the blackboard, 'Well done, Sergeant Butler,' referring to the Frankfurt raid. They had been the ones receiving my signals when I had been in touch with the station and before and after I had gone onto the distress frequency over the sea. They had also been monitoring my signals as I came over the sea pressing the 'O' emergency key and giving the different positions. So they were giving me a slap on the back, which I must say to receive from your peers was really an acclaim in itself. I was very pleased about this.

I mentioned my crew when I first joined at the OTU, and it was more or less quite by accident that we all got together. I suppose in many ways it was the luck of the draw whoever you got in your crew and whether they would all come up to expectations or not. We were all new to each other and you just hoped that it would all work out according to plan.

I would just like to say this about my crew. Without any shadow of a doubt I was a very, very fortunate man to get the crew I got. We didn't look any different from any other crew, there was nothing exceptional about us, but it worked out, right from the pilot through to the rear gunner.

The pilot, Harry Locke, made a great captain of the aircraft. He was a good leader, he was steady under any sort of emergency, and he did his job exceptionally well, giving the right commands. He also had a good sense of humour, was a good disciplinarian and we were a good crew under his command.

Then up front we had the bomb aimer. Frankie Townsend was a great member of the crew. He was a very friendly, affable bloke. He carried out his role very efficiently and knew his job. He was good on the Mark 20 bombsight, he could handle all his equipment and he was steady under fire, if you like. Both Frank and the pilot, Harry, were 23 years old, the same age as myself.

Then we had the engineer, Bill. He looked a little bit on the frail side sometimes. When he first joined I wondered how we were going to go on, but he made a smashing member of the crew. He did his job excellently. It was very complicated with all the dials and switches, and he had to assist the pilot on take-off, landing and with the general handling of all the fuel, etc. He was always there if anything was needed, always able to oblige and deal with matters. He was also the same age as me.

Then there was Horace Hassall, our navigator. At 33, he was the old man of the crew, but what a magnificent navigator he was. There was none better on that squadron than him. He could handle whatever situation came along, no matter what kind of emergency. If we had to deviate because of flak ahead, or whatever, he always had a course to steer, never any problems. He would immediately vary the course and tell the pilot what course to steer.

As for myself, I think they all had plenty of confidence in me. I did my job fairly well, I think. We all did our jobs well.

We didn't have a regular mid-upper gunner, so then we come to Tommy Munro, the rear gunner. He was a great bloke. He was the next oldest at 31 – a little bloke but tough as hell. I always had a good time with Tommy – we used to pull one another's legs. He was a great rear gunner, very conscientious indeed. He was always cleaning his guns, oiling them, etc. His equipment was always immaculate. We all had every confidence in him on raids.

So that was our crew and I was very proud and pleased to be a member of it.

That was almost 70 years ago. It doesn't seem that long, but I can remember it all still so vividly.

Our rear gunner, Tommy, eventually moved to Australia. The pilot, Harry Locke, used to go down and stay with him near Swansea when he was on holiday because he was over here from Australia and had no relatives to visit. He and Tommy had quite an affinity. While Harry was over here he met a girl in the local village near where Tommy lived and married her just after the war. I went to the wedding – all the crew went – and she moved to Australia with him after he was demobbed. Tommy went out there a year or two later with his wife and they went on to have a family of four or five lads.

It was about 1955-56 when Tommy went there. A year or two later we had word from his wife, Joanne, that he had died suddenly. I never did find out exactly what the cause of his death was, but he was only about 45 or 46. That was one member of the crew gone, leaving only five of us.

The next unfortunately to go was Bill. He used to arrange all our reunions when we used to meet up, from about 1955 up until some time in the 1960s. He was working in an engineering firm and had not been there long when he was moving some machinery with an apprentice, and an overhead crane was holding the machine in position. He undid the bolts and, unfortunately, the whole lot fell on him and he was killed. We'd had some good times at the reunions, and Bill was the enthusiast who used to organise it all, so it was very sad. That left just four of us.

Soon after that Frank Townsend, the bomb aimer, decided to emigrate to Australia. His only son, Frankie, had gone a few years before him and his wife. It wasn't a long way from where Harry lived. So he moved over there, leaving just Horace Hassall, the navigator, and myself. We used to meet as often as we could, toing and froing and getting together, and if there were any family celebrations such as weddings we would invite each other. This went on for a good number of years. He died a few years ago. He would have been about 82 at the time, but he developed cancer and I went to his funeral. It wasn't long afterwards that his wife died as well. Now the only one over here who I have any contact with as far as my RAF career is concerned is his son Brian, the eldest of all the children of the crew. He often gets in touch and passes on any bits of information he has heard from various sources connected with Bomber Command, 467 and 463 in particular. When I lost my logbook in the 1950s, Brian managed to get me a replacement. It had belonged to Frank, our bomb aimer, and Brian was given it on a trip to Australia to meet with family members of our crew. It was the same as mine, apart from one operation that was flown while I was in hospital, and I was very pleased to get it.

A few years ago I had word that both Harry Locke and Frankie Townsend had died on either side of Christmas, leaving me as the sole survivor.

Every year, as well as Remembrance Sunday, there are memorial services on Anzac Day (25 April), and I am a member of the Association. There were two squadrons that went back to Australia, but after the war they were disbanded. The members in Australia and those in England have a memorial service at Waddington church and one at the RAF station every year for all the members of the two squadrons – 467 and 463 – who were killed. The people who were left after the war formed the Association, part in Australia and part in England.

We meet at Waddington on Remembrance Sunday and have a short service at the monument outside the church, and also on the camp, as well as on Anzac Day. To the Australians and New Zealanders, Anzac really represents the battle at Gallipoli, Turkey, in the First World War where they were badly beaten and lost a tremendous number of troops. They always make a big day out of Anzac Day in Australia and we accordingly do the same at the camp. We usually have two services. One is outside the local church where a lot of the members from Australia paid for a clock to be erected near the memorial in the church wall. Sometimes we get a fly-over by the one Lancaster that is still flying. We then go to the RAF Waddington camp into the memorial garden, where we have a propeller as a monument to the fallen. We then go and have a meal in either the sergeants' or the officers' mess, after which we also have our annual meeting. Often we'll talk about those we have lost during the year, but, as time goes by, I can't say we particularly discuss Bomber Command. There are very few people of my age from the war there now – the numbers are well down. Very often the people who go are the relatives of the crews that flew during the war, but the majority of crew members, I am afraid, have passed on.

It was unique to be a member of Bomber Command. We were small in number for what we did, in comparison to a lot of other forces, but you felt you had achieved something. To have had the fortune to live through it was really something, an education in itself. It sort of gave you a lot of confidence and the ability to mix anywhere.

I do miss the camaraderie. Crews in Bomber Command were unique. Every crew was like a family, ours in particular. As a crew they kept together, did their training together and their eating and drinking together. They went out as a family, even around the camp. Most of them even died together.

I was glad to switch back to normal life, though. We had had enough of wartime; it was nice to come back to peacetime and know that you were safe. It was an episode in your life that you were proud of but you were glad when it was over. I had some wonderful times with them all and will remember them with pride.

A post-war reunion with crew members. Left to right, they are Bill Holt (flight engineer), Louis, Frankie Townsend (bomb aimer) and Horace Hassall (navigator).

POSTSCRIPT

Louis Butler received the DFM from King George VI at Buckingham Palace in 1945. He didn't visit London again until June 2012 when his lost comrades in Bomber Command were finally recognised for their bravery by the unveiling of a monument in Green Park. He was very keen to attend this ceremony to pay homage to his many friends who didn't return from those raids 70 years ago.

Appendix 1
Operations flown by Sqn Ldr Locke's crews with 467 and 463 Squadrons

467 Squadron

Name	Position	Air Force	Comments
Sqn Ldr Locke, H. B. DSO DFC	Pilot	RAAF	Posted to 467 5.5.43 Posted to 463 25.11.43
Sgt Holt, W. G. DFM	Engineer	RAF	
Sgt Stewart, J. A.	Engineer	RAF	23/24.8.43 only
Flt Sgt Long, A.	Engineer	?	22/23.8.43 only
Sgt Rosen, A.	Engineer	RAF	22/23.11.43 only
Flt Sgt Townsend, F. F.	Bomb aimer	RAF	
Sgt Brown, A. C. F.	Bomb aimer	RAF	16/17.7.43 only
Sgt Hassall, H.	Navigator	RAF	
Fg Off Norris	Navigator	RAF	25/26.6.43 only
Sgt Butler, L. DFM	Wireless operator	RAF	
Sgt Miller, W. S.	Wireless operator	RAF	22/23.11.43 only
Sgt Champ, F. J.	Gunner, MU	RAF	
Sgt Croll, A. J. A.	Gunner, MU	?	22/23.6.43 only
Flt Sgt Simbert, R.	Gunner, MU	RAAF	23/24.8.43 only
Flg Off Proctor, D. W. A.	Gunner, MU	RAAF	4/5.10.43 only
Flt Sgt Munro, T.	Gunner, tail	RAF	

Date	Target	Aircraft	Comments
23/24.5.43	Dortmund	ED547 PO-M	
25/26.5.43	Düsseldorf	ED547 PO-M	
27/28.5.43	Essen	ED547 PO-M	
29/30.5.43	Wuppertal	ED547 PO-M	
21/22.6.43	Krefeld	ED530	
22/23.6.43	Mulheim	ED530	
24/25.6.43	Wuppertal	ED530	
25/26.6.43	Gelsenkirchen	ED530	
28/29.6.43	Cologne	ED534 PO-R	
3/4.7.43	Cologne	ED534 PO-R	
8/9.7.43	Cologne	ED534 PO-R	
9/10.7.43	Gelsenkirchen	ED534 PO-R	
12/13.7.43	Turin	ED539 PO-V	
16/17.7.43	Cislago	ED538 PO-O	Crash-landing in North Africa
7/8.8.43	Genoa	ED530	
9/10.8.43	Mannheim	ED546 PO-W	
12/13.8.43	Milan	LM340	
17/18.8.43	Peenemunde	LM340	
22/23.8.43	Leverkusen	ED546 PO-W	
23/24.8.43	Berlin	ED546 PO-W	

22/23.9.43	Hanover	ED657 PO-N	
27/28.9.43	Hanover	ED657 PO-N	
2/3.10.43	Munich	R5868 PO-S	8¼-hour flight
4/5.10.43	Frankfurt	ED657 PO-N	Attacked by fighter; incendiaries jettisoned and returned to base
22/23.11.43	Berlin	JA902	

463 Squadron (formed 25.11.43)

Name	Position	Air Force	Comments
Sqn Ldr Locke, H. B. DSO DFC	Pilot	RAAF	Posted to 463 25.11.43 Posted to 97 PFF 11.3.44
Sgt Holt, W. G. DFM	Engineer	RAF	
Flt Sgt Townsend, F. F.	Navigator	RAF	
Sgt Hassall, H.	Bomb aimer	RAF	
Sgt Butler, L. DFM	Wireless operator	RAF	
Sgt Brook, T.	Gunner, MU	RAF	
Flt Sgt Munro, T.	Gunner, tail	RAF	

Date	Target	Aircraft	Comments
16/17.12.43	Berlin	JA902 JO-D	
14/15.1.44	Brunswick	EE191 JO-F	
27/28.1.44	Berlin	ME614	

APPENDIX 2
EXTRACT FROM 463 SQUADRON OPERATIONS RECORD BOOK, NOVEMBER 1943

SECRET

Place	Date	Summary of Events
WADDINGTON	27.11.43	Fog on the 'deck' all day prevented the return of the crews diverted after yesterday's air operations. Those personnel remaining on the Station made valiant efforts to get their respective sections and offices organised, and it was observed that great initiative was displayed by many in the noble art of 'scrounging', and it was indeed amazing to behold the amount of furniture and fittings acquired from un-named sources, especially in these times of depleted supplies and equipment
		Pilot Officer Trimble arrived this evening to join the newly-formed 'B' Flight.

Place	Date	Summary of Events
	28.11.43	Visibility again poor, but the mist cleared sufficiently later on to enable our diverted aircraft to return to base from Downham Market at about 19.00 hours.

There being 'NO OPS' again to-day, the boys had a 'thrash' in the mess to celebrate the promotions of Flying Officer Martin to Flight Lieutenant and Flight Lieutenant Locke to Squadron Leader. All crews reported a good 'prang' in the mess, with vast areas of 'devastation'! |
| | 29.11.43 | No Operations again, but two of the younger crews did a spot of night flying, much to the disgust of the ground staff!

Two new crews arrived to join organisation – Flying Officer Leslie and Pilot Officer Heap, both of whom come to us from No 209 Squadron. |
| | 30.11.43 | In spite of continued lack of aircraft and crews, aerodrome lighting and telephones, we are sending three crews to visit Nazi-land. The captains – Flying Officer Leslie, Pilot Officer Heap and Pilot Officer Roberts.

Operations later cancelled, so we sent Flight Sergeant Bowman and his crew on a Bulls-eye, while the rest of us return to our respective messes. Much publicity gained for the new Squadron as a host of reporters descend like birds of prey upon us. No doubt the already horrible lines shot by many 'Aussies' will be greatly magnified by these representatives of the press.

Up to this date 26 crews have reported, so No 463 Squadron feels that it does now actually <u>exist</u>! The Captains are: P/O Heap, P/O Trimble, F/O Leslie, F/Lt Vowels, F/Lt Mortimer, P/O Wilson, F/Sgt Merrill, P/O Foster, P/O Cooper, P/O Hart, F/O Schultz, Sgt Bowman, P/O Baker, F/Sgt Fowler, P/O Kell, F/L Martin, S/Ldr Locke, Wing Commander Kingsford Smith, P/O Smith, P/O Nancarrow, F/O Fayle, F/Sgt Saunders, P/O Schomberg, P/O Messenger, P/O Dunn, and P/O Roberts. Of these, one is now reported missing, having failed to return from the first operation; this is, of course, F/Sgt Fowler's crew.

H. B. Locke S/L
for Wing Commander, Commanding
NO 463 (RAAF) SQUADRON |

Above Louis Butler today.

Below left Louis's angels! During his 90th birthday celebrations in 2010 he was photographed with all his granddaughters, (left to right) Elizabeth, Ashleigh, Marie, Kathryn and Susan.

Below right Co-author of this book, grand-daughter Susan Claire Butterworth.

Above Louis's daughter Vivienne Oxley stands beside the 2005 memorial to the aircrew who lost their lives flying from RAF St Eval.

Below The ancient church at St Eval, dedicated to St Uvelus, was the station church for RAF St Eval for about 20 years. In 1989 a memorial was dedicated to mark the 50th anniversary of the RAF presence, which included this stained glass window in the Lady Chapel.

Above Ann and Louis Butler share a bench at Waddington in May 2010, with their daughter Christine Butterworth beside them.

Right A portrait of Ann taken in 1942 in the uniform of the County Police. She and Louis were married for 67 years until her death in 2011.

Above Louis stands in front of the memorial board at Waddington in 2010. His medals, from left to right, are the Distinguished Flying Medal, the 1939-45 Star, the Aircrew Europe Star, the Italy Star, the Defence Medal, and the 1939-45 War Medal.

Left Standing beside Louis is Brian Hassall, son of the crew's navigator, Horace Hassall.

70 years on: on 28 June 2012 Bomber Command was finally acknowledged for the sacrifices made by its crews during the Second World War when Her Majesty Queen Elizabeth II unveiled a magnificent memorial in Green Park, London. It forms a 9-foot-high bronze of seven airmen in a stone dome, and pays tribute to the 55,573 crew members who lost their lives during the Allied bombing raids over Germany between 1939 and 1945. Louis was determined to attend the unveiling to pay tributes to his many lost comrades.

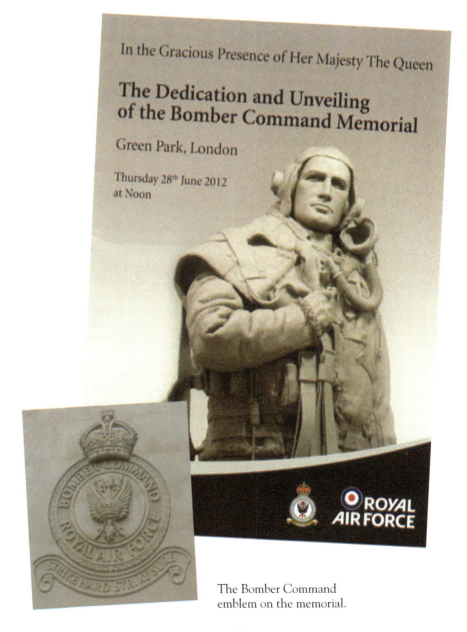

The Bomber Command emblem on the memorial.

Above On the previous day an event was held at the Guildhall, London, and here Louis sits in front of the privately owned forward fuselage section of a Lancaster, with its Disney-esque artwork. The 21-foot-long section was discovered in a Manchester scrapyard some years ago and has been refitted with many original parts.

Left Louis at the entrance to Green Park with his three daughters, Vivienne Oxley, Christine Butterworth and Angela Hobson. *Keith Collman*

Above Louis enjoys a lengthy discussion at Green Park with Air Chief Marshal Sir Glenn Torpy, retired.

Below Meeting Camilla, Duchess of Cornwall.

Above Family members in the hospitality tent: from left to right, Christine (daughter), Louis, Kathryn (grand-daughter), Kathryn's husband Peter, Elizabeth (grand-daughter), and Vivienne (daughter).

Below Louis showing his medals to his grandson Calum Barnes (sitting right), sons-in-law David Butterworth, John Oxley and Stuart Hobson, and grandsons-in-law Peter Stanley and Mark Bardsley.